The 10 Phases of No

CANADA'S
JESUS REVOLUTION

Charlotte Quist

CANADA'S JESUS REVOLUTION
Copyright © 2014 by Charlotte Quist

Scripture marked NIV taken from the Holy Bible, NEW INTERNATIONAL VERSION®. Copyright © 1973, 1978, 1984, 2011 by Biblica, Inc. All rights reserved worldwide. Used by permission. NEW INTERNATIONAL VERSION® and NIV® are registered trademarks of Biblica, Inc. Use of either trademark for the offering of goods or services requires the prior written consent of Biblica US, Inc. Scripture quotations marked NLT are taken from the Holy Bible, New Living Translation, copyright ©1996, 2004, 2007 by Tyndale House Foundation. Used by permission of Tyndale House Publishers, Inc., Carol Stream, Illinois 60188. All rights reserved. Scripture quotations marked KJV are taken from the Holy Bible, King James Version, which is in the public domain. Scripture quotations marked MSG are taken from The Message. Copyright © by Eugene H. Peterson 1993, 1994, 1995, 1996, 2000, 2001, 2002. Used by permission of NavPress Publishing Group. Scripture quotations marked AMP are taken from the Amplified® Bible, Copyright ©1954, 1958, 1962, 1964, 1965, 1987 by The Lockman Foundation. Used by permission.

Printed in Canada

ISBN: 978-1-4866-0703-7

Word Alive Press
131 Cordite Road, Winnipeg, MB R3W 1S1
www.wordalivepress.ca

Cataloguing in Publication may be obtained through Library and Archives Canada

CANADA'S
JESUS REVOLUTION

"...Yet who knows if you have come to the Kingdom for such a time as this?" Esther 4:14

Bless You as You take Your place in Canada's Jesus Revolution!

Charlotte Bol

CONTENTS

INTRODUCTION

GOD IS STIRRING THE CHURCH IN CANADA TO RISE UP, TO BE AN active part of His plan for national transformation. A Jesus revolution is the vehicle by which that transformation will occur. Such a revolution is the key to unlocking Canada's prophetic destiny.

Recently, I was preparing a set list for leading a worship event. As I sifted through the massive list of potential songs, I found myself drawn to a particular theme. Over and over this theme came up in the lyrics. Song after song contained the same core truth. It was the anthem of awakening—more accurately, it was the anthem of revolution.

My spirit leaped as I read lyrics that said "there's an army rising up" and "a generation takes its place." The theme continued with words such as "revival hearts on fire" and "this is our battle-cry." Over and over a message of movement, action and confrontation resounded; the soundtrack of revolution had been released.

The music provided a perfect melodic accompaniment to the prophetic cry of my own heart and the hearts of so many others across this land. The time is now. From north to south and east to west, the message is clear—the sound of awakening has given birth to a call for revolution—a Jesus revolution for Canada!

The reality of revolution hits hard. That single word "revolution" can stir up so much in our hearts and minds. If we are to embrace it fully, we must know that the call to revolution is perfectly and powerfully wrapped in truth that is repeated in God's Word and is fundamental to the victorious walk of the believer. It is a truth that seems to have been somewhat forgotten in recent years, a truth that must be taught, engaged and experienced by the Church of Canada in this hour.

That truth is that *God always wins*!

Consider the words of the Apostle Paul regarding the battle of the Church:

> *Put on the whole armor of God, that you may be able to stand against the wiles of the devil. For we do not wrestle against flesh and blood, but against principalities, against powers, against the rulers of the darkness of this age, against spiritual hosts of wickedness in the heavenly places. Therefore take up the whole armor of God, that you may be able to withstand in the evil day, and having done all, to stand.*
> —Ephesians 6:11-13

He says we do not fight against flesh and blood but he does *not* say that we do not fight. On the contrary, God has equipped us for war. We have been given armour, weapons, power, authority, and, most importantly, marching orders from the King of Glory.

The battle cry is far more than it might initially appear. It is not about personal agendas, self-gratifying platforms or human wishes. No, the battle cry is actually the Spirit of God calling His Church to live fully the life He has given us. It is a call to lay hold of the victory that Christ has won for us. The battle cry is a call to pursue the heart of the Father and then live out the desire of His heart here on Earth. It is a cry for the lost in our nation. Church, we have been called to be salt and light. We hold the key to the change that Canada so desperately needs.

As we pursue the Lord together through this book, which is based primarily on the story of Esther, I pray that you will experience a greater awakening and a revelation of the destiny call on your life. I pray that you will receive strategies, prayer directives and specific action plans to fulfill your mission at this time in this land.

"…Yet who knows whether you have come to the kingdom for such a time as this?" (Esther 4:14)

You are called to be part of Canada's Jesus revolution!

CHAPTER 1
THE AWAKENING

NATIONAL TRANSFORMATION. AWAKENING. CALL TO ACTION. Activation. Rise up. These words and phrases must be the words on the lips of the Church across Canada in this hour. God has sent out a call across the land from sea to sea. It is a call to action, a call to battle, and a call for the Church of Jesus Christ to rise up and take her place.

But what does this call really mean? Where do we fit? What will it cost us? What purpose will it serve? Will it work? Where do we begin?

Some of us have been hearing the call for decades, while others have heard it only in the last year or two. For still others, this call is brand new. In any case, what matters is that we have been awakened and that now, in our increasingly alert state, we are beginning to wonder why. Why were we asleep? Why are we now awake? What does God have planned? This is a great position to be in. If we are willing to seek, God will make certain that we also find the answers He provides.

The fact that you have picked up this book today is telling. Your interest indicates the pull of the Spirit of God on your life. He has given you a hunger for revolution and transformation. He has given you a desire to see Canada changed by the power of the living God. God has generated this hunger in you to guide you toward your destiny. You are called to something far greater than you know.

I would guess that you have been feeling a heightened awareness about what is happening to and through the life God has given you. There is an indefinable restlessness in your spirit. There are questions rising up from deep within—questions that have not been part of your thinking patterns in the past. This is the subtle nudging of the Holy Spirit.

Perhaps you've been contemplating Canada's destiny and what role, if any, you are meant to play in it. You have been questioning your purpose and the impact of your life here on earth. You find your mind travelling down the path of "what if?" What if I lived somewhere else? What if I lived at another time? What if I were somehow different? These questions quickly lead you to ask more direct questions: Why here? Why now? Why me?

Let's take a moment right at the beginning to dig into those questions a bit more. Consider the words of the Apostle Paul in the book of Acts:

> *From one man He made every nation of men, that they should inhabit the whole earth; and He determined the times set for them and the exact places where they should live. God did this so that men would seek Him and perhaps reach out for Him...*
>
> —Acts 17:26-27, NIV

God knows exactly who you are and has determined where you should be and when you should be there. He is purposeful about the times and places of your life. According to the words of Paul, God placed you where and when He desired. He wanted to give you the best possible chance of finding Him and living according to His eternal design for His eternal purposes.

Many people mistakenly think that we are simply lucky to have been born into a wealthy, free nation, that we are fortunate to live in this moment of history. Not true. These ideas miss the big picture. God has positioned you and me here and now to accomplish His purposes. We have been blessed with much and therefore much is required of us. We do not need to feel guilty about living in a first-world nation but neither can we fall into the temptation of slumber. We must stir our hearts to reach for Him and ask Him why.

Let's consider your placement in life for a moment. You live somewhere, belong somewhere, and are part of a kingdom, nation, dominion or some other classification of governmental authority. Rulers and leaders serve in positions of authority in these governments, and therefore these same people, at least in part, govern factors that affect your life. This creates a connection between their life and yours. Their lives and their choices have outcomes that affect your life and your reality.

Have you ever considered that your life might also be able to have an effect on theirs? Have you considered that the awakening that God has activated in your life might serve a greater purpose in the awakening of the nation?

Have you considered the possibility that the awakening that God has done in your life might serve a greater purpose in the awakening of the nation?

God positioned you in Canada now, at this moment in history— for His purpose.

Perhaps you feel that you are well out of the reach of governmental power and authority. Your life may be lived far outside the spotlight of the leaders and policymakers of the land, but God has still called you to have an impact. He sees what we don't see. God has called you for such a time as this, and He will cause your voice to be heard. Your life matters, not only to the people in your immediate sphere of influence, but also to people across the nation, and yes, even to the leaders and rulers around the world. I speak a great spiritual truth when I say that their success depends on *you.*

I'm sure we have all heard the saying that everything rises and falls on leadership. As the king goes, so goes the kingdom. The world has seen both good and bad leaders take positions of power and has witnessed the effects of their rule in the lives of the people they govern. But what does this mean for those of us who are not the king? How can we ever affect change if we are not the Prime Minister, the President, the Premier or even the chairperson? Are we forever destined to simply accept and live with the consequences of the decisions of men and women in authority? Are we powerless? Not according to the Bible. We, the Bride of Christ, have the ear of God. God holds the heart of the king in His hand and He will turn it as He desires (Proverbs 21:1). We are in relationship with the all-powerful Master of the Universe—Adonai.

Powerlessness is a lie from the enemy of our soul who loves it when we believe we can do nothing. He uses such lies to bait us. Powerlessness is one of the greatest tortures a mind can face. It is against our natural, God-given design. When we feel helpless or powerless in a situation, we instinctively try to remedy that feeling. Our enemy knows this. Satan's response is to offer us the lies of false control and escapism (which the Bible often refers to as slumber). He knows that if we try to wrongfully seize control, we will cause damage. He also knows that if we choose escape, we will disengage and shut down to the point of numbness. Either response will block us from realizing our true identity and calling.

When we look to the original creation in the Garden of Eden we can clearly see how God delegated authority. God gave humankind authority and power to steward the earth. It is true that this authority was relinquished to the enemy after the Fall of Adam and Eve but it is also true that it was fully redeemed for us by the Second Adam, Jesus Christ.

As men and women of God who are new creations in Christ, we have been given power and authority once again. The all-powerful Master of the Universe has created people to walk with Him, to rule with Him, to be the vessels by which His Kingdom comes and His will is done on earth as it is in heaven. We function in the visible realm, operating as extensions of Him who is unseen.

We function in the visible realm as extensions of Him who is unseen.

We are carriers of His authority on earth and we are charged to function as men and women of influence in this world.

We are *not* powerless. On the contrary, we, as men and women of God, are carriers of the Kingdom of God. We are ambassadors for the King of kings and the Lord of lords.

For many decades now we have seen an alarming turn within the nation of Canada and indeed throughout many nations of the world. Wrong belief systems and behaviours, previously thought impossible, have become commonplace. We hear of atrocities against the young and the old alike. Our core values of faith and family have been challenged, ridiculed and marginalized.

In the media, we watch a never-ending stream of corporate wrongdoings, scandals, socially repugnant behavior, murders, suicides and all manner of illegal activities.

We have relegated God to being a "higher power of your choosing." In fact, many young people grow up today thinking that God doesn't exist or that somehow they themselves *are* God.

We have reduced the family to being a simple group of people of any gender or sexual orientation who happen to care for each other. We have legalized the right to kill babies in the womb and call it "freedom." We have stripped away the sanctity of life, the gift of childhood and the assurance of a dignified, honourable conclusion to our earthly days. We have become obsessed with living to extremes and we fight anything or anyone that would dare to suggest boundaries. We have become a nation that has very little of its former identity still intact.

Where once we, as a nation—and most especially as the Church—would have been shocked and appalled, we now sit and simply wonder what's next. The reality of what we see and hear is horrifying, to say the least. The leaders of our nation have allowed and sometimes even caused this breakdown and therefore we, the "regular people," feel powerless to change it.

The feeling of powerlessness has lulled many within the Church, to simply disengage and to settle into a type of passivity through the comforts, freedoms and privileges we enjoy. We have bought into the lie of the enemy and have chosen a spirit of escapism. We have denied the power God has given to us and we have been asleep. We are not dead, weak, incapable or insufficient—we have simply been asleep. Truthfully, for many years I was asleep—but no more. God has sounded the wake-up call. He has awakened me and I believe He has awakened you too.

As you read this, you may wonder whether I'm some kind of a radical. Already I've challenged some pretty sensitive issues. But there is an important distinction to be made: I am not called to attack what is wrong; rather I am called to declare truth and champion what is right. The fire of truth burns within me more and more every day.

The call of the King has gone forth. He is commissioning His Bride. He is asking her to stand and be counted, to be a light in the darkness, a city on a hill. And yes, perhaps these words seem radical, but radical action and radical love are required in the hour of revolution.

I don't judge people, and I don't stand on a platform of hate or intolerance—that isn't God's way. But the lie of powerlessness has been found out. Now is the time for the sons and daughters of God to be revealed. I believe with all my being that the righteous love of God will no longer allow His name to be slandered nor His children to be made captive by the false kingdoms of the world.

Our nation and many of the nations of the world are at a desperate tipping point. I believe God has begun to build a fire in the hearts of His people, a fire that cries out, "Enough!"

We can no longer stand idly by while wrong is called right, and right is called wrong. We can no longer be silent as children are murdered, and false "truths" on public platforms dictate our behaviour. We can no longer listen as officials try to convince us to focus on the rights of robbers, abusers, liars and thugs—while outside the spotlight, the Church is having her rights and freedoms stripped away. We can no longer reminisce about the days when our children could pray at school and share the love of Jesus with their friends. No. We can't wish for what was. Rather, we must begin to earnestly anticipate what will be. We must rise up and take our place in the Jesus revolution.

As Christians eagerly awaiting the return of Christ and our eternal home, it is tempting to fall into an escapist mentality. "Come, Lord Jesus" is our cry, as it should be. But our voices should also be heard lifting a cry for the lost and broken, a cry for justice and a cry for a generation in desperate need of a Saviour. We have been commissioned by Jesus Himself to walk in the fullness of His anointing and reach out to the world around us.

We can easily be duped into believing that there simply is no other way for things to change other than the return of Christ. But we must remember that Christ is coming back for His Bride *"that He might present her to Himself a glorious church"* (Ephesians 5:27). Glorious means splendid, noble, magnificent and illustrious. When Christ returns, the Church will not be a weak, emaciated, impotent, frail thing simply holding out until her rescue comes. No! She is called to be powerful, holy, magnificent and indeed glorious.

If you are still reading, I believe your heart burns as mine does. The cry of "Enough!" is on the tip of your tongue. You have struggled at times wondering whether you are intolerant, insensitive, old-fashioned or irrelevant. You have questioned whether there is any chance for a change in this nation at all.

But you have also begun to recognize the lie of powerlessness, and you've begun earnestly anticipating some sort of divine breakthrough. This, once again, is the stirring of the Holy Spirit. This is part of the birthing of revolution.

You have been called, along with countless others across this great nation, to step out from the masses. You've been called to walk in supernatural love and mercy, to be compassionate, kind and gracious, and to manifest all the fruit of the Spirit as an ambassador for God.

You have also been called to raise a war cry. You have been commissioned by the King of Glory to contend for change. You've been called to activate His Kingdom come and His will done on earth as it is in heaven. You feel that fire burning in your heart today because you are called to be more than simply a ransomed soul—you are called to be a revolutionary!

Prayer

God, I have heard the wake-up call. I have seen the desolation around me and I have heard the cry of the lost. But it is not just their cry I hear, O God. I hear Your cry, Your call to action, Your declaration of freedom. I admit that I don't fully know what all this will mean for my life but I commit myself to You.

God, I am Yours.

CHAPTER II

THE CALL OF THE REVOLUTIONARY

MANY OF US FIND THE WORD REVOLUTIONARY TO BE A BIT intimidating. There are not too many happy images connected with this word. Most of us have visions of historical dramas where bloodied bodies, ravaged by the effects of revolt, lie amidst destroyed buildings and tattered flags. We can see the battlefield with the eyes of our mind and we know a great tragedy has occurred in the name of rebellion or perhaps liberty.

The truth is that many times we recall history through the distorted filter of movies, stories and legend. In reality, the revolutions of the past (though indeed bloody and harsh) were often great acts of love. Such revolutions have proven to be historically significant turning points for many nations of the world. They represent a cry for freedom that rose in the hearts of men and women, one that was declared from the rooftops.

Revolutions are historical markers that show us what can happen when a group of people rise up with courage and boldness to reach for something better than the life they have been living.

History's truly great revolutionaries were people motivated by not only the cry of their own lives but also those of the next generations. These revolutionaries were men and women who had grown tired of what had been. They dared to dream of a better way of living; they were ordinary people ready to lay their lives on the line to bring about a revolutionary change for all.

Much of history has taught us to equate revolution with rebellion, but this equation does a disservice to the memory of the revolutionaries of old. The mobilization and subsequent actions of revolution are not at all the same as rebellion. The differences are found in both the motive and the driving force fuelling the fight. Understanding the difference helps us take the mental leap we sometimes sense is required to embrace God's revolutionary call upon our lives.

A rebellion is an uprising or revolt. It is an action or extension of the demonic spirit of rebellion, an open opposing and reviling of authority. It is an ugly and unrighteous thing. Everything about a rebellion fights against the Spirit of God on the inside of the person who is born again (1 Samuel 15:23). It feels wrong because in God's eyes it is wrong. God is all about authority and so we know that rebellion is not His way.

In fact, God has a lot to say about authority. He teaches through the words of the Apostle Paul:

> *Let every soul be subject to the governing authorities. For there is no authority except from God, and the authorities that exist are appointed by God. Therefore whoever resists the authority resists the ordinance of God, and those who resist will bring judgment on themselves.*
> —Romans 13:1-2

But if God is opposed to rebellion and to the overthrowing of authority, then why are we talking about revolution? Because, revolution is by definition a vastly different matter. Revolution is simply a means or a method to a life-altering, reality-shifting change.

> Revolution is simply a means or a method
> to a life-altering, reality-shifting, change.

Though revolution often brings a change in the authority structure and the people within that structure, it does not necessarily mean rebelling against authority. There are methods and systems of revolution that take on a very different form than that of rebellion and war. Revolution done God's way and by His strategy is all about love. It is motivated by the nature of our Father. A God-directed revolution has the ability to bring a change in all things while still respecting the authority of those who govern. It recognizes Almighty God as the supreme authority and it respects the authorities He has put in place. Godly revolution cannot go against the character of God nor can it fail to honour His heart.

Let's take a moment to look at the true definition of revolution in order to broaden our understanding. According to the Merriam-Webster Dictionary, the definition of revolution includes the following: *a sudden, radical, or complete change; a fundamental change in political organization; activity or movement designed to effect fundamental changes in the socioeconomic situation; a fundamental change in the way of thinking about or visualizing something: a change of paradigm.*

These definitions make it clear that a revolution does not have to be a rebellion or a violent fight against authority. A revolution is simply the enforcing of a change, a new way of living. By extension, a revolutionary is not someone who walks in rebellion, but rather someone who brings about change. A revolutionary is someone willing to become a catalyst for the stripping away of what was and the ushering in of what will be.

Jesus the Revolutionary

Catalyst for change? That sounds like Jesus to me. Jesus never lifted a sword, fought against government or picketed for change. Jesus did not incite the masses to revolt or fight for change by any natural means. In fact, many people had a hard time believing that Jesus was the Messiah because they were expecting a king on a warhorse who *would* fight. Instead, they met a man with the nature of a shepherd who loved and inspired people with His words and deeds. But contrary to what a casual glance might indicate, Jesus was far from passive and His revolution was not without conflict. In His short thirty-three years on earth, He forever changed the world. Jesus turned ways of thinking upside down, and brought freedom to a hurting world by God's divine methods.

Jesus was indeed a revolutionary. Note the words He spoke when he stepped into the temple to share from the Torah:

> *The Spirit of the Lord is upon Me, because He has anointed Me to preach the gospel to the poor; He has sent Me to heal the brokenhearted, to proclaim liberty to the captives and recovery of sight to the blind, to set at liberty those who are oppressed; to proclaim the acceptable year of the Lord.*
> —Luke 4:18-19

If these words of Jesus (quoting the prophetic declaration of Isaiah 61) aren't the words of a revolutionary, then I don't know what would be. He used this public opportunity as a defining moment of self-identification. Jesus stood before the leaders of His day and, at great risk to His own reputation, put Himself on the line. This was only the beginning of His ministry and already He was declaring what His life was about. He was declaring that He was more than Joseph and Mary's son. He was more than a carpenter. He was more than the average guy everyone thought He was. He had come to change the world.

In this moment, Jesus shook reality with His words. He said that He had come to bring good news to the poor. He was about to heal the brokenhearted and bring sight to the blind. Perhaps one of the most revolutionary things Jesus said was that He was proclaiming freedom to the captives and bringing liberty to those who were oppressed. These were words that challenged people's understanding of reality. Jesus was declaring a change of everything that they knew and were familiar with. He was saying that people could no longer dictate who was bound and who was free. He was declaring that true freedom was a state of the heart—that freedom was God's to declare. People didn't have to live sick, defeated, oppressed lives anymore. Jesus stood in the temple and very calmly declared a complete paradigm shift. He declared the Good News!

Many times when we read these words of Jesus, we skim them or casually mumble them. The subtlety of the moment of Jesus' declaration disguises the massive importance of what actually occurred. Modern readers may miss the powerful impact that those words would have had on all those present in the temple that day. The power of Jesus' words can be seen just a few verses later when the men rose up in anger as they tried to throw Jesus off a cliff outside the city. Why were they angry?

We have to look closely to see the strong message His words contain. They are powerful and life-altering. We must allow ourselves to feel a sense of the passion and love that compelled Jesus as He spoke. This was no casual reading of Scripture—this was a moment that all of history had been waiting for.

Imagine if you will for a moment, the scene in the movie *Braveheart* when William Wallace, with wild hair blowing across his blue war-painted face, yells *"Freedom!"* Masses are stirred by his passion, and the enemy is both shaken and enraged. The cry thunders in the heart. It calls forth the warrior in each viewer. It inspires honour, courage, truth and justice.

Now let me assure you that the political and religious rulers in the temple with Jesus quaked no less at His declarations. In fact, I believe all the powers of the spiritual realm shook as Jesus stood up and in effect declared a new day—a dawn of revolution.

Perhaps you can see that there is a revolutionary cry in the words of Christ but you might wonder what it has to do with us. The answer is everything! This is our identity: our lives are hidden in Him.

We who have been bought by the blood of Jesus now have no life of our own. We who have been set free are now called to set others free. We who have heard the Good News are now called to live the Good News and proclaim it to others.

I know that as you read this today you feel a stirring of your heart. You know there is a mission. You believe that there is more to living the Jesus life than simply being a nice moral person. You can feel the warrior on the inside of you begin to stir—many of you have been feeling it for a long while already.

Some of you may have begun to tell others of your missional thoughts and been ridiculed. Don't worry: not everyone understands revolutionary living yet, but they will. The shifting seasons in our nation will soon demand it.

The call of Almighty God has gone forth across our land and the words "*Wake up!*" can be heard echoing through the Body of Christ.

The call of Almighty God has gone forth
across our land and the words "*Wake up!*" can
be heard echoing through the Body of Christ.

His words reverberate in the caverns of our inner self. You have heard it. Revolution is at hand.

The concept of a Jesus revolution can only be fully grasped by one who has been awakened. It must be filtered through an embrace of the cross and a complete surrender to the great love of Jesus. Consider what Scripture has to say about life:

For the love of Christ compels us, because we judge thus: that if One died for all then all died; and He died for all, that those who live should live no longer for themselves, but for Him who died for them and rose again.

—2 Corinthians 5:14-15

I have been crucified with Christ; it is no longer I who live but Christ lives in me; and the life which I now live in the flesh I live by faith in the Son of God, who loved me and gave Himself for me.

—Galatians 2:20

And he who does not take his cross and follow after Me is not worthy of Me. He who finds his life will lose it, and he who loses his life for My sake will find it.

—Matthew 10:38-39

You see the call to life in Christ is a call to death. We are called to die to self and rise to a new life in Him—an eternal life with eternal purpose. This life is abundant and free and is designed to be shared. Embracing all that God has for us will require that we release all that we presently hold. We must be willing to lay it all on the line. We must be willing to put ourselves out there to be His hands and feet. We must be like the apostle Paul who said he was compelled by love (2 Corinthians 5:14).

How can we embrace the gospel and not desire to see the Good News proclaimed to those around us? How can we walk in freedom and not seek freedom for our friends and family? How can we have our eyes opened and not minister to the blindness all around us?

The slumbering Bride in Canada is in the early stages of awakening. She is just now beginning to look around and truly understand what is going on around her. As her eyes are opened, she is discovering that we have come to an unprecedented place in history. Never before—except perhaps in the days of Noah—has the world been in such a state of despair.

As our spiritual eyes adjust to the dawn of a new day, we see a generation that is desperate for the hope and truth of the gospel. It is as though everything has been turned upside down while the Bride slept. It is time for the truth to come forth and turn things right-side-up once again.

There are no answers to be found in natural wisdom. We have exhausted the scope of what humanity can solve on its own. The more we try to fix things, the worse they get. Unfortunately, many (if not all) of these issues have arisen as our society has turned away from its foundation of faith.

If we take a moment to look through Canada's history, we can easily find evidence of a nation that was founded on the principles of the Word of God. Sadly, in just a few short decades, we have become a nation that now barely allows the name of the true God to be declared publicly. We have seen the wisdom of God be replaced with human theories and the ideologies of secular belief systems. Where God-fearing men and women once forged policies, laws and even nations, now many Christians find themselves feeling hopeless in the face of strange political jockeying and rapidly changing societal norms. We have gone from being the plowmen of new frontiers to passive sheep awaiting rescue. Our nation is groaning and we, its people, are bearing the fruit of this failing.

The enemy craftily lied to us about our identity and lulled much of the Church to sleep. While we have slumbered and closed our eyes to the realities of evil, our adversary has been gaining ground. But the wake-up call has sounded. The rescue is here. What's really exciting is that you and I are called to be part of it! You are called to wear a new title. You are called to be a bearer of truth. You are called to be a revolutionary.

Revolution vs Rebellion

Once again, it is important that we remember the difference between revolution and rebellion. Without this distinction firmly in place, we will not succeed. Recent history has shown us what rebellion will do. We can easily see the grave effects of what surely must be a counterfeit freedom. Rebellion and revolt will only lead down a path that is rooted in the very foundations of evil.

Our society today is living the effects of rebellion against God's authority, governmental authority, spiritual authority and family authority. We see what the enemy camp brings and we can see how it so successfully destroys. Jesus said *"The thief does not come except to steal, and to kill, and to destroy. I have come that they may have life, and that they may have it more abundantly"* (John 10:10).

This is the nature of Jesus' revolution. It is strategically designed to take the effects of rebellion and turn them on their end. It takes the death and destruction of the enemy and declares life instead. Not just any life, but abundant life! This is what happens when God rules—life pours forth. We lay down our life and receive instead an abundant overflowing life of love that is no less than miraculous.

One aspect of a revolution is the replacing of one leader with another—one of the people's choosing. As the Church has been roused from her slumber, we feel an urgency of heart to see God take His rightful place as ruler of our nation once again. A nation can be turned right-side-up only under the rulership of the rightful King. He alone can do what needs to be done.

But the change of national rulership is the result of a national revolution, and a revolution is facilitated by men and women who will allow themselves to be revolutionaries. These revolutionaries must be people revived by the Spirit of God, with hearts on fire for the Lord. These aren't rebellious dissidents but people compelled by love and a cause. They are compelled to see freedom of the captives, eager to see His kingdom come and His will done on the earth. People compelled by a passion for the one true King.

Prayer

God I come before You today in response to the wake-up call in my heart. I believe You have called me to more than ordinary existence. I don't want to live for myself any longer. I want to really and fully live for You. God I believe You have called me to be salt and light in this very dark world. You alone have power to make things right in this land once again. I thank You that light dispels the darkness and that You are the light in me. So today, Lord, I say "yes" to You. I say "yes" to Your call upon my life. I open myself today, Lord, to hear my marching orders from You. Give me a heart that beats like Your heart. Give me compassion for the lost and hope for the salvation of this generation. God I surrender to Your will.

I am Yours!

CHAPTER III

SECRET AGENTS & SACRED STRATEGIES

HOW ARE PEACE-LOVING PEOPLE SUPPOSED TO UNDERSTAND revolution and national up-ending? We have been taught to love peace, follow peace and to be governed by peace. But there is a vast divide between peacekeeping, and peacemaking. The Church has been called to the latter. According to Matthew 5:9, it is a blessed thing to be a peacemaker.

The stirring of revolution can feel somewhat overwhelming. As Canadians, we've been raised in a culture of peace, calm and safety. We do not have the military culture that we see in so many other nations of the world. We've been conditioned to be polite, unassuming and, frankly, somewhat passive. Canadians are famous around the world for being nice, gentle, naive and easy to be around (or perhaps I should say easy to "push around"). It is often assumed that we lack the courage or strength to fight back—an assumption that has allowed us to slide under the radar in many global conflicts.

I identify with this Canadian persona. I am well known for apologizing for pretty much anything. When someone bumps into me, I apologize. If someone steps on my toe or nudges me with their shopping cart, I take the blame. In fact, when I was in high school, I played basketball and earned quite a reputation for my apologies. I loved the aggression, speed and competitiveness of the sport. I was never very good at getting baskets, but I was excellent on defense. Not much could get past me—as a result many girls got shoved or pushed over as they attempted to score. Although I was well versed on the role of my position and always deeply gratified that I had blocked a shot, I almost always apologized to the girl I shut out. It was my instinct.

It was on the basketball court that I first experienced this inner battle. Although I was polite, apologetic and generally kind, I was also a fighter and I thrived on the challenge and the battle. Basketball showcased the diversity of inner strengths. Graciousness was and still is commendable but so too is strength. There is great value in a fighter when a fight is required.

How many Canadians can admit the same sort of duality? I would guess quite a few. A quick look at such things as our aggressive hockey culture is very telling of our secret identity. In a far more militant example, Canadian soldiers have an exemplary history on the battlefield. Triumphant battles fought in such places as Dieppe, Juno Beach, and Ypres in both World Wars showed Canadians to be a courageous, bold and formidable force.

We may be kind, compassionate, and gentle but we are far from weak. God has placed great strength in our hearts and wrapped it in mild packaging. Our actions are simply camouflage, hiding our true inner identity. We are often underestimated and indeed we underestimate ourselves, but the truth is still the truth. Under our kind Canadian smiles and our easy apologies lay the hearts of pioneers, survivors, explorers and revolutionaries.

The Precedence of Partnership

This concept of dual identity reminds me of the story of Gideon in the book of Judges. The story tells of the oppression of Israel, a nation being bullied and dominated by a people who felt entitled to what was not theirs. The Midianites came, season after season, and plundered the land. They took the best of everything for themselves while leaving a meager existence for the people of Israel. Here's how it is described: *"So Israel was greatly impoverished because of the Midianites, and the children of Israel cried out to the Lord"* (Judges 6:6). Israel had been stripped of everything that would allow them to thrive and increase as a nation.

But the second half of the verse marks a turning point: when the people of Israel cried out to the Lord, they invited Him into their desperate situation. From that moment on there was a shift and God could move. And He chose to move by calling out the real identity of an ordinary man.

Now the Angel of the Lord came and sat under the terebinth tree which was in Ophrah, which belonged to Joash the Abiezrite, while his son Gideon threshed wheat in the winepress, in order to hide it from the Midianites. And the Angel of the Lord appeared to him, and said to him, "The Lord is with you, you mighty man of valor!" Gideon said to Him, "O my lord, if the Lord is with us, then why has all this happened to us? And where are all His miracles which our fathers told us about, saying, 'Did not the Lord bring us up from Egypt?' But now the Lord has forsaken us and delivered us into the hands of the Midianites." Then the Lord turned to him and said, "Go in this might of yours, and you shall save Israel from the hand of the Midianites. Have I not sent you?"

—Judges 6:11-14

Let's dissect this passage a bit and learn a little about the strategies of God. First, notice God's answer to the cries of a nation. Israel reached out to God and He reached out in response. He is never inattentive to our cries and He was not inattentive to theirs—although He responded in a way that was quite unexpected. His response came in the way of an encounter with a man. God's rescue started with a conversation with an ordinary man through whom He would perform extraordinary things.

Let's think about that for a moment. Wouldn't it have made more sense for God to have simply rained down hailstones to destroy Midian? Perhaps He could have created an earthquake or a tornado that would have wiped them out? But He didn't. He chose a simple, ordinary man. God works with people. He partners with people. Partnership with willing and obedient men and women is *always* part of God's strategy.

Far too often, we cry out to God for an answer, desiring an intervention of sorts, without realizing what we are saying. We need to realize that a request for help may be answered with a call to action.

God has always wanted relationship. When we come into right standing with Him through salvation, we experience the birth of that relationship. Our prayers have not simply activated some magical helpline but rather we have invited Him to live in and through us. Prayer draws on that relationship. When Israel cried out to the Lord, He responded with an action plan that required co-labouring with Him—a relational answer. God brought about the victory but He used human vessels to do it.

The second thing we need to appreciate is the first phrase God spoke to Gideon. He said *"The Lord is with you, you mighty man of valor!"* Wow! In this phrase we read the words that revealed divine destiny in the life of a seemingly ordinary guy. It shows that God knew something about Gideon that even Gideon himself didn't know. God always knows who we really are. He knit us together in our mother's womb. He fashioned us and placed in us all that we would ever need to fulfill the dream He has for our life.

Sometimes circumstances and life experience shape our identity into something that really isn't true. But it seems true to us, doesn't it? We are experts on the topic of ourselves. We know how we respond to situations. We know what we have or haven't done, and we think we know better than anyone else what we are capable of, but this is actually false. God knows us in a way that no person on earth could ever know us.

In Gideon's case, the word of the Lord came and activated the truth of his real identity.

This identity is almost like a secret persona in a spy story or a war movie where seemingly ordinary people living very ordinary lives are far more than they appear to be; their real identity is disguised. They are undercover agents planted in situations where they can blend in and wait to be activated at the appropriate time. Sometimes the waiting period stretches long enough that a person might almost come to believe his or her own cover story. They might even seem to forget all the training and preparation, but there will come a time when they are called upon to stand up in their true identity.

In the dialogue between the Angel (God) and Gideon, there is no doubt that God knows who Gideon really is. God calls out Gideon's true self, not saying, "This is what I would like you to try to be," but rather identifying the extraordinary within an ordinary person.

This story is very much like the Canadian situation. I believe God has placed much more in us than we realize. We may feel that we know all that is and is not possible for our lives. Perhaps we believe we are insignificant, ineffective and ill-equipped to do anything great for God. But who does God say that you are? It is in this revelation that destiny is found.

Who does God say that you are? It is in this revelation that destiny is found.

This leads us to the third important element in Gideon's story where God says, "*Go in this might of yours, and you shall save Israel from the hand of the Midianites. Have I not sent you?*" (Judges 6:14) Go in this might of yours. Does it seem possible that God actually thought that Gideon had the physical strength to destroy the marauding thieves?

The key is found in the final sentence: *"Have I not sent you?"* God knew that Gideon was completely unable to do anything without Him, but He also knew what Gideon was capable of when he partnered with God.

Partnership with God was the key to Gideon's step into the miraculous. Gideon was a mighty man because he was dependent on God. He was weak and unable to do it on his own but this made him mighty because it caused him to be fully reliant on God. The Apostle Paul experienced this same phenomenon when he wrote, *"For when I am weak, then I am strong"* (2 Corinthians 12:10). What makes us great and able to do great things is not ability or talent but rather the willingness to be a conduit for the power of a great God. It's as though we have a void that becomes a sign and a wonder when filled by God. The true source is always God and the glory always belongs to Him.

Consider if you will the concept of electricity. Electricity is a constant that powers a multitude of different devices. When electricity flows to a lamp, there is light. When it flows to an iron, there is heat. When it flows to a refrigerator, it produces cold.

Are you following what I'm saying? The appliance or tool itself is useless without power but each item has within its design the potential to fulfill a specific purpose when supplied with power. A refrigerator is still a refrigerator even when it is not plugged into a power source. However, it doesn't really become useful or functional as a refrigerator until it is connected to the power supply.

People are designed in the same way. Our true identity and design does not become evident until we are connected to the power supply of God. If the power is removed, so too is the ability to function in the proper way. Gideon was indeed a mighty man of valour but no one knew it until he connected with the power of God. His identity didn't surface until it was activated by God. The power was in the partnership between

Gideon and the Lord. Gideon was a conduit God chose for the release of His mighty, rescuing power.

> *For you see your calling brethren, that not many wise according to the flesh, not many mighty, not many noble, are called. But God has chosen the foolish things of the world to put to shame the wise, and God has chosen the weak things of the world to put to shame the things which are mighty; and the base things of the world and the things which are despised God has chosen, and the things which are not, to bring to nothing the things that are, that no flesh should glory in His presence.*
> —1 Corinthians 1:26-29

Powered for Purpose

God loves the fact that you don't think you can do it (whatever "it" is for you). He can work with a lack of natural ability—in fact, He's looking for it. What we can do without God is rarely, if ever, glorifying to God. If we feel confident that *it* is in us, then it is also probably of us and for us.

God knows what He has put in you and He knows your real identity. He knows what will be possible if and when you partner with Him and allow Him to move through you.

Willpower alone will not cut it. Drive, ambition, education, networking or upbringing will never be enough to carry out the plans of God in your life. He is looking for willing, empty vessels who will allow Him access to their life.

God can use the simplest person to amaze and penetrate the most learned mind. He can use a humble, broken person to cut through the facade of the strong, rich and brave to deposit truth. Honestly, when we read through Biblical history we very quickly find out that God loves to choose very ordinary people and do extraordinary things through their lives. He picked Moses, Joseph, David, Elijah, Deborah, Peter, Paul, Philip and Mary.

We don't have time for a full history lesson here, but if you study any one of these people, you will find that what they have in common is that they were very ordinary, insignificant people. You will also find that, in their weakness, they were willing to allow God to use them to do something world-changing and paradigm-shifting. Each one of these people, along with Gideon, was a revolutionary in their own time.

How about you? Are you empty enough to be filled by God? Are you willing to be used? Are you brave enough to ask God what He sees in you?

We started this chapter talking about the facade surrounding Canadians. I can't help but wonder what God has placed under the surface in the hearts of His people in this nation. Who are we really?

Even a quick overview of our country in this hour will reveal that we have been pillaged and plundered by the enemy much like Israel was in the days of Gideon. The Canada of today is not the Canada once dreamed of, nor is it yet the Canada that God plans for it to be.

We have been driven undercover and have watched as the enemy has stolen our identity, threatened our society and plundered our land. We have been harassed and tormented by the demonic realm, and we have been fooled into thinking that the best thing we can do is to quietly, passively wait it out. Certainly we have powerful heroic tales in our history books as well—but for the most part we have heard the lies and underestimated ourselves. We have learned to be gentle, peaceable and submissive, and the enemy is content to have us remain that way. It's not that these characteristics are wrong but there is more to be seen. We have had enough. Like Gideon, we have begun threshing the grain in the winepress.

There is something under the surface that is a war cry for this generation. I believe Canada is being called out in this hour to live her great prophetic destiny. We have a purpose to fulfill on the global stage. God is reminding us in this new day that we've been made for more.

Canada is being called out in this hour to live
her great prophetic destiny. God is reminding us
in this new day that we've been made for more.

Canada's Foundation

A study of the history books of our nation and a reading of the Scriptures that Canada is founded on makes it clear that we have been set in position for influence on an international scale. Our nation was founded on God, by God and for God. He has fashioned it according to His design to fulfill His purpose.

Take, for instance, the phraseology used in the full name of our country. We are not called a kingdom, a country or even an empire—Canada is a dominion. Our nation was named the "Dominion of Canada" in reference to the psalm which says *"He shall have dominion also from sea to sea, and from the River to the ends of the earth"* (Psalm 72:8). This Scripture is not just a token reference but is forever documented as a foundational principle of our country. The words of this psalm have even been engraved on the east window of the Peace Tower in Ottawa, our centre of government. On the south side of the Tower is inscribed *"Give the king thy judgments, O God, and thy righteousness unto the king's son* (Psalm 72:1, KJV) On the west side of the tower, we find the words *"Where there is no vision, the people perish"* (Proverbs 29:18, KJV).

Canada is represented by a flag of red and white. Those looking through spiritual eyes see and understand that this is no accident. Our nation is meant to be marked by the blood of Christ and His righteousness. We are called to be a holy nation, a land ruled in righteousness.

Canada is also the only nation with a leaf on its national flag. Canada is known worldwide for the maple leaf. Once again, the eyes of the spirit do not see with a natural perspective. In the Apostle John's revelation, God speaks of such a leaf, *"The leaves of the tree were for the healing of the nations"* (Revelation 22:2). This is our prophetic destiny as a nation. We are called to be messengers of healing and restoration, carriers of hope to a broken and hurting world.

Our national anthem, O *Canada*, contains the words "God keep our land, glorious and free." This is a prayer of dedication that goes forth at most official public gatherings. Many socially conscious people are fighting to have these words removed in light of our present godless culture but God will not be removed. He has been invited in and He wants to rule His nation.

It serves us well to remember that the Word of God is a vital part of all that this nation was founded on. Those who fight against a godly society forget our true identity. Canada has been dedicated to the Lord. His truth, His word was declared from the beginning. These declarations have been woven into the foundations of our nation and they will not be erased. They hold a deep sense of purpose and destiny, a destiny that has been long awaited and almost forgotten at times—almost forgotten by us, but never forgotten by God.

I believe the Spirit of God is saying that the time of revolution is now. The Bride has been awakened to hear the Word of the Lord.

Could it be that God is simply looking for those who will stand up to be used? Could it be that He is looking for the Gideons of our time to step out and begin threshing the spiritual grain and withstand the enemy? Could it be that He is looking for a people who are ready to cry out with the prophet Isaiah *"Here I am, send me"*?

Prayer

God, I come before You today and I ask you to show me what You see in me. Who is it that You have designed me to be? I desire to know my true identity in You. I am well aware of the places I fall short of what I think is required. I thank You that what I see is overruled by what You see. I declare today Lord that I believe You want to use me for Your glory and I thank You that You never intended for me to do it on my own. I believe that when I am weak, You make me strong. Where I am lacking, You supply more than enough. I believe that You are the God of the impossible and I believe that You want to do impossible things through me. I believe, according to Your word, that You are far greater in me than he that is in this world.

Lord I lay down my excuses right now, in Jesus' name. I lay down my own concepts of who I am and what I can do. I choose instead to look at what You can do.

God, You are more than enough and I surrender to Your plan and your ways!

I am Yours!

CHAPTER IV

KINGDOM STRATEGY

AS THE TITLE OF THIS BOOK INDICATES, THERE ARE TEN IDENTIFIABLE phases to a Jesus revolution. These ten phases are the required elements of a very specific strategy that I believe God is highlighting for His purposes in Canada, in this hour. But please know that this is not a how-to book for producing a man-made revival. These phases are not steps to manipulate a move of God. Rather, the phases are a Spirit-led outline, identifying the processes of this particular plan.

We are called to partner with God in His Kingdom strategy. Identification of the phases will help us fulfill our role in the partnership with accuracy and efficiency. And although we have an important part to play, we are not the heroes of the story. We must keep in mind that this move of God is about the character and desire of the Father far more than it is about us. We do not engage in a Jesus revolution because of simple concern for our nation; we engage because God has called us. Our focus, our desire, our motivation is our God.

The ten phases detail the plans and methods of God as outlined in the Word; they bring clarity and understanding about how He moves. When we understand the phases of the plan, according to His design, we are better equipped to identify where we fit in the greater picture. They teach us how to align ourselves with what He wants to do. God has designed the Jesus revolution to facilitate nation-changing transformation.

Before we dive into it, I would like to give you some of the background for what you are about to read.

Background Story

I am a product of the '80s and '90s—which could be called the "self-help" generation. I grew up with a myriad of talk shows, self-analysis books, fitness videos, and self-help programs. There was a do-it-yourself solution for every problem one could possibly face. There were abundant educational tools with three steps to this and eight ways to overcome that—a plethora of programs to help you fix it all by yourself. But I longed for more. I needed an answer from God for the issues of life. My heart cried out for something beyond what human wisdom could provide.

After years of reading, trying and eventually quitting so many different systems for so many challenges, I had come to a place in my own life where I simply was done with human-based concepts. It seemed to me that everyone thought they had found a solution to help them deal with their own personal issues. These solutions appeared to work for them but not necessarily for everyone else, and not always for the long term.

We had the answers for everything and yet somehow, we had solved nothing. As far as I could see, the more we learned, the less we knew. I began to wonder why. If humanity had become so educated and enlightened, then why did we seem to be increasingly undone and broken? Why did we seem unable to come up with a lasting solution for the problems of our society?

The questions drove me to my own foundations of faith. I had been a Jesus-lover almost all of my life—I had grown up in the Church—but it was time for a deeper revelation of truth, time for my grown-up choice to pursue Him with my whole heart. I decided that God was either Ruler of everything or Ruler of nothing. He was either all-powerful or He had no power at all. My heart told me that if God was indeed the All-Powerful Ruler of the Universe, then He alone had the answers I was seeking. He alone held the only real remedy for the ailments of society. All the philosophies and human strategies could never compare to the wisdom of God. I knew in my heart that if the creation was broken, then the only real solution would be to ask the Creator for help.

In the shifting of definitions of truth and the rapidly changing wisdom of the world, I chose to believe that what God said was the final word—it was and is absolute Truth. I chose to live my life based on His Word as my final answer. This is where abundant life is activated.

The choice to embrace Him as the Truth was personally transformative. Let me tell you, I firmly believe there is no better place to live than in Him! There is great comfort and peace in knowing that there is indeed absolute truth. And there is indescribable blessing to be enjoyed by choosing to live as the King commands. My life was transformed. I experienced more abundant life than I had ever known before.

Unfortunately, it was in this place that I let my guard down: I forgot to be alert to the spiritual landmines. I began to thoroughly enjoy God's peace, joy, favour and blessing. This enjoyment moved into a wrong form of satisfaction and contentment. My family and I were experiencing the goodness of God. We were enjoying the fulfillment of His Word in our lives. Unfortunately, somewhere along the way, that became enough. I was comfortable. I was happy. I was blessed.

It became easier and easier to look away from the aching brokenness that existed all around me. I began to forget that the heart of my King was for the lost and dying—that He would leave the ninety-nine to find the one. My blessings were blinding me.

My story is not unique. It is a common tale in the Canadian Church. Comfort can become addictive. We can easily lose sight of the big picture—the Kingdom picture. This is an early warning sign of slumber. If we are not alert, the enemy of our soul will use contentment and comfort as bait, leading us to the trap of complacency and slumber. It is one of his most effective first-world strategies—and it is one of the ways the slumbering Bride came to exist.

The Apostle Paul said, *"for I have learned in whatever state I am, to be content"* (Philippians 4:11). It is important for us to note that he was speaking about the circumstances of life and not the state of his heart. He was content with much or with little, but no circumstance would change the fire that burned in his heart. He was focused on the eternal picture. The Apostle Paul burned for the lost and for the advancement of the Kingdom. He spent every day of his life doing the work of the Gospel. He was poured out in service to his King.

When I speak of contentment being a warning sign of slumber, I speak of contentment of the soul that begins to affect the heart. Blessing is from God and comfort is a tremendous gift, but when we allow these things to affect the temperature of our heart, we have succumbed to deception. The gifts God gives do not negate the commands He gives. The comforts He provides are not a replacement for the Great Commission.

The slumbering Bride is not what some may think it is. Some believers think that because they love God and faithfully serve in the church, they can't possibly be asleep, but that is the subtle deception. Consider the words to the church of Ephesus in the book of Revelation—a church that would fit the definition of a slumbering Bride:

> *I know your works, your labor, your patience, and that you cannot bear those who are evil. And you have tested those who say they are apostles and are not, and have found them liars; and you have persevered and have patience, and have labored for My name's sake and have not become weary. Nevertheless I have this against you, that you have left your first love.*
>
> —Revelation 2:2-4

Slumber is not about walking away from God, rebelling against Him or refusing to be active in service. Instead, it is seen in a Church that is busy in service, but inwardly focused, and somewhat ineffective in impacting the world. A slumbering Church is far more interested in results than relationship with the King. It can be recognized by such phrases as "I don't have time for that," "What am I going to get out of it?" and "I don't really have a desire to do that."

The slumbering Bride has quite simply forgotten that her heart should beat in sync with the heart of her King. She should be moved by what moves Him. Her first love has grown colder and her focus has shifted away from her eternal purpose. She has become engulfed by experiencing and surviving the here and now.

As I was awakened out of my own form of spiritual slumber, my eyes were opened. I began to look beyond my own life and ministry. I began to see the world outside my own nearest and dearest. Suddenly I realized that I had been seeing very dimly for quite some time. I had taken on a type of tunnel vision: my focus had turned inward. It had been far too long since I had really looked at the world beyond my own bubble of blessing, far too long since I had allowed my heart to beat with the compassionate heart of my King, far too long since I had wept for the lost and broken or ached for those without hope.

Don't get me wrong. It's not that I didn't care about the rest of the world but simply that I didn't see how I could do much to change it. It was easier to look at the things that I could control, the people and situations that I knew how to handle. I was fully engaged in serving God and the people inside the four walls of the church. My gaze and my heart had been turned away from the desperation of a nation under siege, a nation that needed Jesus.

I had come to be consumed with busyness within the Church. There was no energy left to even consider the struggles outside—at least that's what the spirit of slumber had been telling me. The problems outside were massive and seemed to be in a cycle that humanity insisted on perpetuating for all of time. How would that ever change? What could be done to help a nation that seemed to be freefalling into despair through acts of humanity's own free will?

The Cycle of Humanity

Ecclesiastes 1:9 says, "*and there is nothing new under the sun.*" Oh, there are new circumstances and new technologies but really the basics of life haven't changed. Humanity has always been relatively the same. We have always had emotions, life experiences, joys, sorrows, friends and enemies. There has always been conflict, anger, jealousy, pride, peace, happiness, gratefulness and love. There has always been God and there has always been an enemy of our soul. This truth of commonality means that history has much to teach us about success and failure. It also has much to teach us about the absence or presence of God in a society and how His presence, or lack thereof, affects each generation.

Psychology teaches that the best indicator of future behaviour is past behaviour. By that measure, humanity is part of a constant downward spiral that will lead to nothing good. You see, in the past, humanity has repeatedly grown and developed socially, intellectually, economically and technologically. In that growth is born the belief that we have arrived, that we've been enlightened and that we have hit the pinnacle of success. It is a very easy leap from there to the belief that we are self-made men and women who have no need for God. From that place comes a very quick fall into complete moral breakdown and societal failure. Proverbs 16:18 prepares us for this when it says, "*Pride goes before destruction, and a haughty spirit before a fall.*"

When we think that we, the created, can do life successfully without the Creator, we have a problem. This is a mountain that mankind has always continued to circle. We circle it and circle it until our cycles of self-glorification become something like the flushing of a toilet that eventually washes our prideful achievement away—only to have another generation follow in our failed footsteps, trying to build something from nothing.

These words may seem melancholy and dark in the light of the great revolution we've been talking about, but it is important to understand why we need a revolution. An understanding of the issue provides a platform for the solution. We don't need an answer unless there is a problem. We won't change unless we recognize that we need change. We will never have the courage to do something new until the pain of staying the same becomes too great. This is the awareness that has been awakened in my own heart and I believe it has in yours as well.

So what kind of problems or cycles am I referring to that might apply to our modern understanding? What issues had I been choosing to avoid while in my slumbering state? They are best seen through the filter of present-day popular culture, both nationally and internationally. We have to take a step back and allow our perspective to take on a broader worldview in order to see clearly. As we do, we can easily discern the downward spiral.

Our society has begun circling the mountain of self-gratification and self-glorification so rapidly that things are spinning out of control. Policies, mindsets and socially accepted ideas are shifting in a matter of months and years, instead of decades and centuries. Our progressive thinking and futuristic ideas have landed us in the same place that Noah found himself thousands of years ago—a society filled with self-glorification, self-gratification and blatant sin.

Perhaps we should consider Sodom and Gomorrah—are those cities so very different from any Canadian city today? What about Egypt in the days of the great pharaohs whose lifetimes were spent building monuments to themselves? How about the Roman Empire? The Romans were so technologically advanced that they had paved streets and running water. Sadly, this Empire was also so morally depraved that it is still famous for its sexual perversion, treachery, murder and general greed and lust for power.

In our more recent history, we might take a mental walk through the stories of the slave trade, the Nazi regime, or the numerous bloody civil wars that have occurred globally in the last hundred years. Humanity always destroys itself—or does it? Who is the true source of the destruction?

One key aspect of absolute truth that I choose to live on is this: God is good and the devil is bad. I take John 10:10 quite literally. I believe that this world is a war zone of sorts and that we (both individually and corporately) are always aligned with one side or the other. With this in mind, a look through the history books seems to prove a pattern: the collapse of a nation and the destruction of a generation occur every time the population chooses to turn away from the One True God. You see, we never really serve ourselves, we serve either The Great I Am or we serve the god of this age. The state of a society reflects the spiritual state of its people. It reflects our relationship with God.

The collapse of a nation and the destruction of a generation occur every time the population chooses to turn away from the One True God. The state of a society reflects the spiritual state of its people.

The enemy of our soul has no new tricks up his sleeve. He is not a creative being so he simply recycles the strategies that have worked in the past. His patterns of action and strategies of destruction have been repeated throughout history. There are, quite literally, stories of atrocities committed during times such as the American Revolution that mirror, with exact detail, atrocities documented in the Old Testament. How could this be unless the same enemy fueled the same blackened hearts of fallen people? When we see the symptoms we can identify the source because the devil's character does not change.

The good news is that although we face the constant attacks of an enemy, there is another constant, a far greater constant—God! We don't have to guess what He will do or wonder if He will show up. We don't need to question His character or His heart. The God we see in the Bible, the God who restored His people over and over again, is the same God we look to for answers today. Consider the following verses:

"For I am the Lord, I do not change"

—Malachi 3:6a

"Every good gift and every perfect gift is from above, and comes down from the Father of lights, with whom there is no variation or shadow of turning"

—James 1:17

"Thus says the Lord, the King of Israel, and his Redeemer, the Lord of hosts: 'I am the First and I am the Last; besides me there is no God'"

—Isaiah 44:6

I don't know about you but when I look at the world we live in, it seems clear that we are on the speedy end of the destruction cycle. I find great hope and peace in knowing that there is a constant God who is still on the throne. It lifts my heart to know that He is not surprised by what is going on nor does He feel overwhelmed by it. He doesn't change. He has always been and He will always be. Best yet, His track record proves His redemptive and rescuing response to the cycle. That track record proves over and over again that God, the Almighty King of the Universe, loves to show Himself strong on behalf of His people. He delights to show mercy and lavish His love on people who choose Him. While our enemy seeks to destroy, God seeks to save, protect, rescue, restore and have relationship with His people.

Let's look at the well-known promise God gave to Solomon, a promise that still applies to us today:

If My people who are called by My name will humble themselves, and pray and seek My face, and turn from their wicked ways, then I will hear from heaven, and will forgive their sin and heal their land.

—2 Chronicles 7:14

God's part in the cycle can be clearly seen in this verse and our part can be clearly seen as well. God never over-rules the choice of the people—He waits for the invitation. If we want Him out, He will stay out; but if we want Him in, He will gladly step in. Notice the phrase *"if My people."* This is not a comment for those who don't know Him. He's talking to His people, the ones who know Him. He's talking to His Church.

Reading a little further we find another truth: our entire nation benefits from our correct choice. It says that He will "heal their land." There is a national benefit to be experienced as a result of the Church taking her place.

This excites me more than I can say. This is powerful! It gives me hope! It reminds me that I am not just a pawn in the life-choices of others, but that I can make a difference because I have relationship with the King of the universe. The promise tells me that the hold-up is not on God's end—it's on ours. "If My people" suggests our will must be engaged. The trouble is not in discovering what God will do; the trouble is in the Church finding what I call "want to."

"Want to" is the result of a wake-up call. It is the response to a realization that something presently exists which needs to change. For instance, it comes when I have a growling in my stomach and I "want to" find something to eat. It happens when I find myself unreasonably tired after performing a task. This makes me "want to" exercise and get into a higher level of physical fitness. Perhaps I have a job interview and find out that I am under-qualified for the position I would like to have. This makes me "want to" take some classes and upgrade my education.

In the same way, in order for me to choose to take part in a national reformation plan, I have to find some reason to want to. We are all this way; it's a function of free will. The "want to" in this divinely marked moment in history is rooted in the awakening of the Bride. Canada's destiny is dependent on the Church being all that she was made to be. The wake-up call has gone forth— we are beginning to hear the heartbeat of our King clearly once again. As we diligently seek Him and learn the desire of His heart, we find our desires coming into alignment with His—we find our "want-to."

Rather than overtly attacking Christians in this last generation, I believe the enemy of our souls has taken the simple warfare strategy of attacking our "want to." He has lulled us into sleep. He has made certain that we don't see or care to see what is really going on beyond our own doors. But no more!

Many within the Church are presently experiencing the aftershock of the season of slumber. We are horrified as we wake up and realize how far our nation has fallen. But this aftershock is a good thing because it propels movement. The awakened Bride is beginning to rise up and step into position.

Wisdom directs us to embrace the sting of the aftershock, for it births a new resolve. Our hearts are beginning to burn. We are being transformed from the inside out—we have chosen to partner with God in the work of restoration and transformation within our nation. We are men and women who are looking to our King to direct our sudden, inescapable urge to do something.

In the last several years since my own wake-up call, I have become increasingly aware of national policies and laws that are nearly unthinkable. I am stunned by the socially accepted ideas of normal behaviour, and am amazed by how quickly they have changed. I almost feel like I'm part of one of those movies where someone has an accident and wakes up from a coma a decade or so later, only to find that their world is no longer the same. I have a hard time believing so much has happened right before my eyes. I am in disbelief that the nation I know and love could have fallen so far while I have been sleeping.

At the risk of seeming insensitive or intolerant, let me share with you a few of the things that are part of my aftershock, things that would have been unthinkable just a few short years ago. I'm sure they are part of your aftershock as well.

In Canada over the last few years we have seen:

- The eradication of God in the public school system.
- The expression "Merry Christmas" become considered offensive and intolerant.
- Easy-access vending machines for drug paraphernalia and condoms.
- Public gatherings endorsing and promoting perversion, anti-semitism, the occult, and all manner of anti-Christ ideologies.
- Genderless public restrooms proposed by lawmakers.
- Yoga become a widely accepted form of fitness and meditation.
- Polygamy and sorcery promoted in mainstream entertainment.
- Scenes of murder, suicide, and abuse shown during family-time television hours.
- Profanity considered acceptable in radio-played music.
- Acceptance and promotion of common-law relationships.
- Legalized gay marriage.
- Legal full-term abortion.
- Very young children being encouraged to decide their own gender identification.
- As many as six different genders being taught by public school systems.

- Young people being encouraged to participate in the use of pornography as a means to sexual education.

This list barely scratches the surface of the shift that has occurred in the very recent history of our nation. This is the reality I saw when my sleeping eyes were opened. This is Canada's present-day, culturally-accepted standard of "normal." Some people see serious problems with every point and some people feel that there is room for a little gray area on some of these issues, but many people see no problem at all.

We must keep in mind that it is not up to any one of us to judge other people but we certainly can observe the actions and judge the fruit. I am not saying that the people who are part of these activities or belief systems are bad people. On the contrary, I believe that every person on the face of the earth is a candidate for the all-encompassing, everlasting love of God. His heart is for each one of us.

This is where the awakening gets a little tricky. None of us enjoys the idea of rocking the boat, but we cannot ignore what we know to be right and wrong. While God desperately loves each and every person, He does not love everything we do. The actions and ideologies being promoted in our society today are very obviously contrary to the design of God and the commands He gave in His Word. Not only does that make the actions offensive to Him but it should make them offensive to His Church as well. What's really interesting is that most of these activities were offensive to pretty much anyone, Christian or not, just a decade or two ago. In one generation, Canada, as we knew it, has been quite literally turned upside down.

If a nation (and much of the world) has changed its paradigm of normal in such a short period of time, isn't it possible that it can be changed once again? If the enemy has tipped it upside down, is God not well able to turn it right-side-up again? It is within this framework that the strategy of a Jesus revolution lays.

As I was awakened by the Lord and had my eyes opened, I must admit I felt somewhat helpless. The aftershock of awakening stirred my "want to" but I lacked any understanding of the "how-to." The issues I saw appeared to be an overwhelming mountain of righteousness that needed to be climbed. Even if the whole of the Body of Christ was to wake up to the truth, what could we really do? How could we affect change? Was it too late? Where would we possibly begin? What was the divine strategy for Canada?

I was still in the process of mulling these things over, and seeking the Lord for answers, when I was invited to speak at a conference whose theme was "calling the Church to its destiny." That phrase burned like fire in my heart. I knew it was a prophetically accurate statement of truth but I had no understanding of where to go with it. The "how-to" was still missing for me.

I thought and prayed for weeks searching for a starting point. I absolutely believed that the wake-up call had already sounded. I believed (and continue to do so) that the answer to the ache of the world is the treasure of Christ hidden in the Church.

The answer to the ache of the world is the treasure of Christ hidden in the Church.

I had always known that the Church is called to be salt and light in a darkened world but again I wondered what we could do. How much power do we really have on a national or international level?

The Revelation of Esther

It was while musing on these questions that I sensed the Lord direct me to speak on the book of Esther. I was not impressed. I was looking for something of a war cry and God was asking me to preach about a beauty queen. It was not where I wanted to go, but I know better than to second-guess God. As I begrudgingly agreed with Him to preach on the beauty queen, I sensed Him say, "If that's what you think the story is about, you are not reading it correctly." So, with open eyes and heart, I decided to give it another read. This led to another read, and another and another.

I experienced a revelation of truth: the book of Esther is not just a simple story about a beauty queen at all. Far more accurately, it is the story of a revolution. It is the story of a fallen government system, a deceived king, a demonic territorial principality, a captive bride, a divine solution and a national reformation.

In the ten short chapters of the book of Esther, we find the documentation of the kind of amazing story that great movies and novels are made of. It has a villain and a hero, a kingdom and a king. It has a love story, a war and a glorious ending.

The remarkable thing is that this story is not a fable. It is not made up for our entertainment; it is actual historical fact. But why did this story make the biblical cut while others faded off into the forgotten past? We know that God did not breathe forth the Scripture for our entertainment, and He was not concerned with simply documenting history. Timothy puts it this way:

> *All scripture is given by inspiration of God, and is profitable for doctrine, for reproof, for correction, for instruction in righteousness, that the man of God may be complete, thoroughly equipped for every good work.*
> —2 Timothy 3:16-17

According to the Word, the book of Esther allows us the great privilege of reading a story that is able to teach, correct, instruct and equip us. Hebrews 13:21 reminds us that when God calls us, He also equips us.

God has called us out; therefore it only makes sense, according to His character, that He will also equip us. In this hour, I believe part of that equipping is found through the divine strategies found in the book of Esther.

In the following chapters, we will walk through the entire book of Esther and pull out the God-strategy hidden within. We will walk through the ten phases of national transformation, the ten phases of a Jesus revolution.

Revolution is a strong word and necessarily so—this is serious business!

Our nation has been broken, battered and held captive by the lies and schemes of the evil one for far too long. It is time that the Lord be given His rightful place as head of the Dominion of Canada once again; He will not share His rule. The revolution is not about removing the power of this nation from the hands of one person to give to another. Rather, it is about unseating the false god that has been plundering our land, and choosing to enthrone once again the mighty King of Glory.

As we walk through these ten phases, you will surely be able to identify which place you are in; I believe you will also see where we are prophetically as a nation. The wisdom and knowledge of God will bring great freedom.

Allow the Word of God to speak to your spirit as you read these chapters. Immerse yourself in His truth. Be changed, inspired, convicted, challenged and empowered by what He has to teach us through the lives of Esther, Mordecai, King Ahasuerus and Haman. It will be life altering if you allow it to be.

Prayer

God, I believe Your Word is truth, wisdom, and life. I believe that You have awakened my heart and called me; I believe that You equip those You call. Today, Lord, I choose to believe that there is equipping for me to be found in these pages. Help me to understand, receive and appropriate Your Word. May Your truth become my reality. I look to You for instruction, oh Lord.
I am Yours!

CHAPTER V

PHASE ONE: FINDING FAVOUR

Please note: The Book of Esther is our accompanying text for this study. Reading the applicable passages in addition to this book will help you more fully grasp the concepts and strategies. Please read the first two chapters of Esther before continuing.

AS WE START DOWN THIS ROAD OF LEARNING REVOLUTIONARY strategy, let me first say thank you for being willing to pursue this. Hunger for change is the proof of an awakened heart.

There are ten phases to study and experience. God is inviting us to do more than simply learn about them—He's inviting us to experience them and to really live them. All ten phases are essential for complete transformation of a nation. The nation will begin to experience the effects of these phases as we each take our place and begin to move.

The phases don't always come in order for every individual, nor do each of them take the same amount of time to be completed. We cannot race through the phases or prematurely step into the next phase. In fact, you may find yourself participating in several phases at once through different aspects of your life and calling, and that is okay.

If you find that you are only at the beginning, celebrate that beginning. Celebrate the fact that you have been awakened and are moving. Praise God! If you find that you have arrived at a later phase, celebrate and know that you are about to experience some very exciting, extraordinary things. Praise God!

The first few phases are foundational to the overall strategy and therefore must be firmly established. If you find that you are personally a little further down the list of phases, you can use these earlier chapters to serve as a checklist to help make certain that you are ready to advance. I assure you it will get far deeper and more exciting as we go along. With every phase we move closer to complete national transformation.

I caution you that the point of identifying and studying these phases in not to rate your progress as a Christian, nor is it to help compare yourself to others. Comparison is a trap of the enemy that cripples advancement. The phases are quite simply a guide to provide perspective. They help us understand where God has positioned each one of us, and provide counsel to help us function fully and effectively in that position.

Individual movement results in a corporate movement. National transformation happens one person and one phase at a time. Our place or phase as a nation may not coincide with the phase you are at personally. Don't worry about that. You are only accountable for your own life. Keep your eyes on your race and run it well. Just be who God made you to be and thrive in the place where He has you in this moment.

Setting the Stage

Let's begin by setting the stage. By analyzing the core ideas, we will easily see the startling similarities between the ancient world of Esther and the one we live in today.

The story of Esther is an epic historical tale occurring around 480 years before Christ. The entire national transformation from start to finish spans a period of approximately ten years. In the great scope of history, this is a remarkably speedy turnaround. At the beginning of the book we read the tale of a self-gratifying, broken kingdom. Just ten short years (and ten chapters) later, we find a God-fearing king who presided over a national revival.

Most of us are familiar with the story of Esther to some degree, but allow me to refresh your memory with an overview of the setting. Esther's story takes place in the kingdom of Persia, which was the place of Babylonian captivity for the Jews in the days of Daniel. At this point in history, the Medes and Persians had overthrown the Babylonians, and the Jews were no longer captives but were still considered some of the lowest subjects in the kingdom.

King Ahasuerus (also known as Xerxes) took over rule from his father in 486 B.C. Three years later, he decided to throw a party of massive proportions for all the rulers and nobility of the land. The purpose of the event was to celebrate his reign, along with the great wealth and vastness of his kingdom. The party actually lasted six months and was followed by another seven-day feast which was for all the residents of the region. This feast was an overwhelming spectacle of wealth and glory. It was designed to show off and parade all that the kingdom had won, plundered, produced and possessed—and it succeeded. The whole event was a tribute to self and a flagrant display of pride.

It was during this final seven-day feast that King Ahasuerus decided that he would add one more trophy to the show. He called for his queen so he could parade her before the officials in the kingdom; it was not enough to show off his belongings but he also wanted to show off his trophy wife, Vashti. And, you know the story—she refused to come.

Vashti's refusal was a huge affront to the king and to all of his officials. Their response provides us with a clear indicator of the national political climate. These officials actually became afraid of the fallout from Vashti's behavior. They suggested to the king that allowing her actions would send a wrong message to all the wives of the kingdom. If Vashti didn't have to obey, then other women wouldn't obey either. The officials were worried that the actions of Ahasuerus would affect their personal lives. Insubordination freaked them out. Fear was a huge factor in the king's court.

In fact, the officials were afraid that there might be an uprising throughout the kingdom if it became known that someone had refused to bow to the wishes and commands of the king. They believed that aggressively responding to the queen's actions would provide the remedy. More specifically, it would force the women of the land to comply with the wishes of their husbands: *"When the king's decree which he shall make is proclaimed...all wives will honor their husbands, both great and small"* (Esther 1:20).

The combination of the festivals, feasts and freak-outs give us a great overview of what the nation was really like in those days. First of all, it was very prosperous. They had the best of everything and seemed to be at the top of their game both in military conquest and domestic fruitfulness. They were prideful and displayed an attitude of arrogance and superiority.

Secondly, the king's reputation and status on the national and international stage was of vital importance to him. This is scary because anytime a ruler cares more about public opinion than personal conscience, there is a gateway that the enemy can use—and he did so here.

The next thing we notice is that the king did not choose to think for himself. He took counsel from his public advisors on matters of a personal nature and allowed their paranoia to shape his decision.

Finally, we see within the fear of the advisors a repulsion for free thought and speech. They felt that by making an example of one person they could control the actions of others. They played the "what if" game, and decided that the queen's refusal to be displayed as property at a drunken feast would in turn encourage rebellion and incite national dilemma.

Let's pause the story for a moment and locate the present-day Canadian connection. We too are prosperous and flourishing. We have and continue to seek to have a good reputation on the international stage. There are advisors to our government that are afraid of anything that would rock the boat. They do not want Christianity or Bible-based values spread out in public because they fear that it would upset other groups within our society. As a nation, we don't like to have anyone become offended. There is a great concern that a small action could create a large mess that would affect everyone. It's easy to see that the same demonic strategies at work in Esther's time are also at work in ours. It's also easy to see and believe that the strategy God used in her day will also work in ours.

As we read a few more verses in Esther, we see that King Ahasuerus came to his senses after a while (a period of approximately three years), and remembered the queen. In other words, he actually missed her and felt a void because of her absence.

At this point, the advisors show up in the story once again. They realized the king was experiencing a loss and they attempted to find a solution. They came up with the idea of a great beauty contest of sorts. They had officials travel throughout the provinces and gather together all the beautiful young virgins. The young women were to be groomed, prepared and presented to the king. He would have the prerogative to choose which one he wanted to crown as his queen.

It was a strangely uncontrolled gathering-and-selecting process, considering the influence any future queen might have. The advisors seemed to forget the great harm they felt Vashti had been capable of causing. In this moment, it became completely about the visual for them; they saw the queen as a simple window dressing. Chosen exclusively for their appearance, these young women came from many different backgrounds and from all parts of the kingdom—with all manner of beliefs, religions, and customs. They were invited into the palace to be prepared, tried, evaluated and finally either selected or rejected. This selection was more about what they appeared to be and less about who they really were.

This selection process holds another interesting similarity to the state in which we find our nation. Canada was founded on Christian principles but, sadly, when we became inflated with wealth and filled with pride in our own achievements, we decided that God wasn't doing for us all that we wanted Him to do. Under the influence of ungodly advisors, a series of decisions were made that have essentially removed God from our governmental systems.

As the years passed we came to a point where we suddenly noticed a void in the fabric of our society. Things went wrong. People lacked hope. The future seemed daunting. So again, under the advisement of the godless, we opened our doors to a huge variety of faiths. We searched high and low, far and wide, to find a god, any god. We have settled into allowing everyone to define God in their own way. It seemed politically and socially correct to encourage people to select the "god of your understanding," a phrase that has been stated on more than one national telecast in recent years.

As awakened Christians, you and I know it is not about finding the god of our understanding that will bring hope and life. No, nothing will change until we encounter the One True God. And God is preparing this nation in this hour for just such an encounter.

Deciphering the Code

As we move forward in the story of Esther, we journey beyond the national situation and move more specifically into a knowledge of the key players. In the second chapter of Esther we are introduced to Hadassah, a young orphan who has been raised by her cousin Mordecai. We come to know her by her Persian name, Esther.

Very quickly Esther moves to the forefront of the story. A surface read tells us that the story is about her; Mordecai almost seems like a secondary character. The perspective shifts drastically when we read the story through Kingdom-strategy eyes. As we do, we find that Mordecai is far more than he first appears to be, and so are other main characters. It is here, in this deeper study, that the buried meaning begins to surface. The stage has been set and now the lesson must unfold. There is Kingdom strategy to be learned.

Understanding the concepts and lessons tucked away under the surface will require us to step beyond the obvious storyline. We will have to dig to see the types and shadows hidden within. Digging below the obvious to discover the yet-to-be-revealed truth may be new for you, but it is a solid, well-established method of biblical instruction.

Consider the parables of Jesus. He frequently used a surface storyline to deliver a lesson with far more impact. The technique of instructing through types and shadows is also frequently found in the teachings of the Apostle Paul, as well as in many instances throughout the Old Testament.

Take, for example, the story of the Beloved and the Shulamite; most scholars agree that the Song of Solomon can be related to the love between Christ and the Church. The story of Jonah in the belly of the whale for three days is a prophetic representation of Jesus in the belly of the earth after the Crucifixion. The poem of the Shepherd found in Psalm 23 is an artistic representation to us of the care of God for His people.

Likewise, within the story of Esther lays a great truth to be revealed. There are four main characters who must be identified for whom they represent. It may not be obvious at first glance, but as we dig through the story, it will become abundantly clear.

Guide to the Code of the Characters:

1. **King Ahasuerus represents a type of national or governmental leadership**

- He is the voice of decrees and decisions that affect all the people of the land.
- He has the authority to make laws.
- He is fuelled by a concern for the kingdom he oversees.
- He is responsible for the outcome of national activities, both good and bad.
- He has advisors that consult with him, but ultimately cannot force his decision.

2. Haman represents a type of demonic principality

- He has no authority or power of his own.
- All of his authority must be given and assigned to him by another.
- He advises the king for his own gain.
- He seeks to possess the land.
- He feels he has a generational right to rule.
- He has a hatred for God's people and seeks to kill, steal and destroy.

3. Esther represents the Bride of Christ, the Church

- She is a foreigner in the land where she lives.
- Her real identity is found in her lineage and bloodline.
- She was adopted by one who was willing to sacrifice his own life for her.
- She is chosen by God and on assignment for Him.
- She is the vessel through whom God's will is performed in the land.

4. Mordecai is a type of Christ

- Mordecai embodies the characteristics of God: compassion, faithfulness, honesty, kindness, wisdom and righteousness.
- He gave of himself to adopt Esther.

- He works behind the scenes in advising Esther to fulfill her mission.
- He was paraded through the city and celebrated (triumphal entry).
- He is personally committed to saving the lives of his people.
- He triumphed over his enemies.

When we look at the powers and forces behind these characters, it becomes obvious that this book is more than a casual glance would suggest, far more than just a documentation of history.

There are many historical stories about a many different people, but not all of them are included in the Bible. God himself has selected the ones that are included. They are divinely anointed to reach out from history to provide wisdom for the present.

Esther's story was chosen by God to serve as an example of national transformation through proper use of the governmental systems. It teaches us how to combat the infiltration and domination of the enemy. The book of Esther is a game plan for transformation and a guidebook to the phases of revolution. It is an invitation for the people of God to rise up, take their place, and see the salvation of their God.

Finding Favour

Let's get started unraveling the mystery by digging into the life of this young Jewish woman, a woman who was favoured by God. It's highly unlikely that Esther felt honoured or favoured when the king's men took her captive. She probably didn't feel favoured as she was imprisoned in the harem of the king—but she was. Feelings don't always show an accurate reading, they must be measured against God's truth.

You may think, as I used to, that her time of preparation was one spectacularly fun year for her. What young woman wouldn't like the opportunity to live like a princess for a year? Who wouldn't want a chance to be the queen?

Sadly, the reality these young women experienced was far from wonderful. None of the women who were selected were ever allowed to return home again. They were ripped away from their homes and families to be "tried out" by the king. If he didn't choose them, which would be the reality for all but one of them, they would be taken to the king's harem. He might never call them upon again. Each of the young women knew that if the king did not choose her, she would become damaged goods with no hope of the future she had dreamed for herself. Their lives were forever changed the moment they entered the palace with the king's men.

According to Scripture, the women spent a year in the king's harem being prepared to meet with him. They went through six months of treatments with oil of myrrh, and then six months of perfumes and beauty preparations. Again, this sounds like a high-end luxury spa upon first glance, but that was not the case.

The six months with oil of myrrh was all about removing what had been. Myrrh was used for its antiseptic and healing properties. The goal was to slough off dry skin, remove sunspots and freckles, and exfoliate any sign of where the women had come from. Myrrh was about stripping away the past life in order to prepare for the new life. That first six months would have been tragic to the young women's sense of identity. The life they had known was scrubbed off, leaving them tender, raw and vulnerable.

Then the second six-month portion of the preparations began. During this time, the young women were perfumed and coiffed and educated to be part of their new world. They needed to look, smell and behave in a way that was pleasing to the king. They were basically moulded and crafted into something completely different from anything they had known before. They were strangers in an entirely new world.

Imagine if you will the feelings that Esther must have gone through. She had been taken from her home, critiqued and criticized for what she had been, then turned into what someone else wanted her to be. She would never go home again to live as Hadassah ever again.

She must surely have known that her chances of being selected by the king were very slim. She was wrapped in unknowns and uncertainties in a world that was unfamiliar and uncomfortable to her.

Esther didn't fully know or understand who she was or where she was going. As we read the story, we see that thankfully even in the uncertainty, she chose to embrace the call of God. She did what needed to be done. She accepted counsel. She walked carefully and graciously into all that she faced. She walked in the wisdom of God.

Notice the description of Esther's experience in the early days of her time in the house of the women. She thrived in the midst of the trial:

Now when the turn came for Esther the daughter of Abihail the uncle of Mordecai, who had taken her as his daughter, to go in to the king, she requested nothing but what Hegai the king's eunuch, the custodian of the women, advised. And Esther obtained favor in the sight of all who saw her.
—Esther 2:15

The king loved Esther more than all the other women, and she obtained grace and favor in his sight more than all the other virgins; so he set the royal crown upon her head and made her queen instead of Vashti
—Esther 2:17

Somehow in the middle of losing her identity and walking into the unknown, Esther had favour. Scripture says she had favour with everyone who saw her. God made a way for her where there should not have been a way: she was given additional beauty treatments in the preparation phase; she was given maidservants from the king's palace to assist her; she was given the best place in the house to live. Following this, she was given favour with the king. He saw something different in her; he delighted in her.

Esther is a type of the Church, which means we too have favour. You see, she could have been caught up in the fact that she was in a difficult place. She could have chosen to focus on her circumstances. She could have fixated on the fact that she would never be going home. She could have been overcome with fear about the unknowns of her future, but she did none of this.

Esther chose to embrace the position she had been placed in, and follow the favour in a nearly hopeless situation. I'm sure she had no understanding at that time that God wanted to use her to rescue a nation, but she trusted God and trusted His plan. Esther understood that she needed to be faithful where she was and follow the favour.

How does this relate to us in our Jesus revolution? Well, *you* are Esther! Phase one is activated when we recognize that God has a master plan, and choose to engage it. The phase is completed when we are positioned correctly, serving faithfully and awaiting further instruction.

We play no real part in God's plan until we are willing to partner with Him and live by His design. The strategy of the ten phases begins for us when we stop living for ourselves and choose to take our place in the divine strategy.

As you say yes to God and embark upon a life of surrender, you may feel very uncomfortable. This surrender may be a first-time salvation or it may come as a result of the awakening, but either way, it must come. Your life is no longer your own: you've been bought with a price. Fullness of life comes with fullness of surrender.

Fullness of life comes with fullness of surrender.

For a time it may feel like life is suddenly turned upside down. The Kingdom plan for your life is based on an eternal realm and may be difficult to rationalize. We must remember that we are called to walk by faith, not by sight. You might feel like you don't know what to do, where to go or who to turn to. You may yearn for what has been left behind and feel anxious about what is ahead. It might seem as though moving forward into the unknown is far too hard. Move forward anyway—it's worth it!

As you step onto this journey, your heart will begin to expand to anticipate the possibilities, you will begin to dream a new dream—a God dream. The next difficulty you will face is waiting. The dream takes time—and it is on a clock that you have little or no control over. You may feel trapped in the great in-between. This phase will take as long as is needed to position you correctly. Don't panic: God is still in control and He has not forgotten you.

You might not like where you are right now, and you may see no way out. You may hate your job, dislike where you live and feel hopeless about your future. You may feel frustrated by your inability to actively pursue the things that are on your heart. Remember the year that Esther experienced. It was difficult for her too, but it was only for a season—and most importantly, God was in it.

You have been awakened. You have been called into service. God has chosen you. It may feel very much like you've been picked up and taken to the palace and there is no way out. It is unknown, scary, risky and intimidating. You won't have all the answers or know all the ways God may move. But you must recognize that, even in this place, you have favour. This is your mission in this phase—find the favour and then be faithful. Get in position.

Favour will show up in the most unexpected ways. It might show up in your job, housing, banking or relationships. Favour will open doors and help you be positioned correctly—you just need to choose to follow it.

One thing to be aware of is that favour is actually not for us. That is, it is not exclusively for our benefit. God gives us favour to serve His purposes in us. It helps us get where He wants us to be when He wants us to be there. Favour is a heavenly positioning system.

Favour is a starting point, not a finish line. Notice the description in Luke 2:52 of Jesus as a young man: *"and Jesus increased in wisdom and stature, and in favor with God and men."* Jesus increased in favour. Favour wasn't the final goal; rather, it was a facilitator of destiny. Favour opened doors and positioned Jesus for His future calling.

Perhaps you are reading this today and you actually feel fully satisfied with your life—and that is a nice place to be. But is there a sense of God's divine purpose as well? Are you alert to the big picture? Are you still moved on the inside by the things that move your King? Are you still fully surrendered?

You may recognize that you have favour and you enjoy walking in the goodness of God. Maybe you love your job, your home and your city, and you are quite content to stay there. If it isn't broken, why mess with it, right? Remember, contentment is good but not at the expense of the Great Commission. Contentment with circumstances is necessary and right, but complacency disguised as contentment leads to slumber. I challenge you to be alert to the false lulling of the enemy. Again, favour is not the finish line.

We must realize that there is always a bigger picture to be considered because we are part of a greater Kingdom. Imagine if Esther had simply been excited, and satisfied that she had favour. What if she thought she had arrived by being made queen? You see, being the queen was not Esther's destiny—facilitating a national transformation through revolution was! The position of queen was simply the tool God chose to use in order to bring about change; it was part of her destiny but not the entirety of it. Esther could have decided that she didn't need to do anything further. She could have just celebrated the fact that God had granted her favour and lived in passive luxury for the rest of her days. Praise God she didn't. This was just the beginning of the story and only the first phase of the overall strategy.

Many Christians today find themselves in one of two false mindsets. The first one is a defeatist mindset. They focus on the circumstances instead of looking for the favour. They get swallowed up in the temporal and miss the eternal.

The defeatist believes that life is not what they had hoped it would be, and they feel rather indifferent to the idea that it might ever change. They long for what was instead of pressing on to what will be. They spend much of their time looking in the rearview mirror. They find it easy to recount the many ways the world is wrong and the multitude of reasons they are helpless to do anything to change it. Quite simply, they are blinded to the divine favour that is available to them.

The second false mindset is that of premature celebration. It views favour as the final win. This happens when we see the favour of God upon our lives, but we fail to recognize its purpose. Again, this is a symptom of looking at the temporal instead of the eternal. It misses the bigger Kingdom reality.

Premature celebrators know they have favour. They can see that they have a voice where others don't. They know they have opportunities other don't have. This awareness is exhilarating and exciting, but it also can be addictive. We can very easily choose to embrace the favour without asking God what He wants to do with it.

Premature celebration manifests in the "us four and no more" mentality that we often hear about. It says things like *"We are so blessed. We are so very grateful to God for the amazing favour upon our lives. It is sad that those other families aren't experiencing it, but that might change if they chose to get right with God."*

These statements are true in a manner of speaking, but they ignore the mission. Yes, others would experience the goodness of God if they knew Him—maybe God has favoured you as a means of opening a door to reach them. Maybe He wants to use you to bring about change so those other families have the opportunity to hear the Gospel. Your favour might be for them.

You see, Esther could have stopped at delighting in the fact that she wasn't banished to the harem; instead she took the position that had been given to her and awaited further instructions. Favour led her through phase one and also the next nine phases, as you will soon read. Favour positioned her in the present and prepared her for the future.

Our job in phase one is to follow favour to exactly the right place at exactly the right time. We must realize that there is a much larger strategy in play, and that we have a role to play in it. We must stop looking at the circumstances of our life as the key to our future—only God holds the key. We must refuse to complain, whine, drag our feet or quit. There is no back door to destiny, so we must stop trying to pacify the flesh by maneuvering with human means. We must find and follow the divine favour.

Try asking God why He has you where you are. Where does God bless you? Where has He made a way for you? Where do you have influence? Ask him for discernment for your daily life. Ask Him about your job, your home, your town, your church, your ministry and your social activities. Where do you see favour?

Find out which of these placements were of His choosing and design and which were of you. Be prepared to let go of anything that is not of Him. Grab on to the things that are of God—embrace them. Choose to be faithful in these areas. See them as the God-designed strategy that they are. Get your eyes on the big picture and then follow the favour.

Your employment is not simply about making money and surviving— it is the place the King has sent you for His purpose. Your home is not located where it is simply because you wanted to be there—God has positioned you for His plan. Walk faithfully in the favour.

It is wise to realize and embrace the reality that God is intimately acquainted with every aspect of your life. He cares. He has a master plan. If you are a child of the King, then you have a position for Kingdom purposes. It has been orchestrated by a far greater wisdom than your own. God has chosen the exact place, and time where you should live, because it is part of His redemptive plan. Trust Him with that.

Nothing in the Kingdom of God is by accident. There is purpose in all that God does. We are called by purpose to live on purpose for a purpose. The sooner we get on board with God's strategy, the sooner we begin to see the next steps and phases unfold in our lives.

Ask yourself: am I where God wants me to be right now and am I doing what He wants me to do? If not, find favour and follow it. Make the necessary adjustments. If the answer is yes, then stand firm, be faithful, and keep your heart fixed on the King—phase one is complete.

Prayer

God, I thank You that You are well acquainted with the details of my life. I thank You that You know who I am and where I am. I am so grateful that You have chosen me to be part of Your plan upon the Earth. Lord, I have found it hard at times to clearly see where I am going or why I am where I am. Today, I come to you to surrender my need to know. I believe You are in control and that You have a plan that is good and full of life. I choose today to stop complaining about my circumstances and to stop trying to maneuver a way out of them. I believe that Your plan works and so I surrender to You. I choose to look for Your favour upon my life and I choose to walk in it fully. I know Your blessing is not for me alone. Help me to embrace Your favour while I keep marching forward with You. Help me to see that I am part of a far bigger plan and give me a heart for those who need You so desperately. Once again, I surrender myself completely to You, oh God.

I am Yours!

CHAPTER VI

PHASE TWO: UNDERCOVER ASSIGNMENT

At the conclusion of Phase One, it seems as if life has been re-ordered and everything is now free to move forward in God's master plan. And it is, but unfortunately it doesn't always look or feel like we think it should. Phase two is not easy. In fact, none of the phases are easy but they each hold tremendous value and accomplish great things, both in the Kingdom and in us.

So how should we approach phase two? Well, to put it in military terms, if phase one is recruitment, phase two is boot camp. Just to make it a bit harder, it is an undercover boot camp, one you may have to face with a certain degree of solitude. It is all about training and preparation for all that is yet to come.

Being undercover serves three very important roles in your revolutionary journey: training, testing and maturing.

When we are awakened to the greatness of the Kingdom plan and we begin to engage it, we often feel like we are ready for action right away. But we aren't—there is much preparation to be done. Only God knows all that we are about to face and He will not send us to the front lines until He knows we are adequately prepared. He sets us up to win. And so, we proceed through phase two— the Undercover Assignment—with anticipation. Our prayer becomes more than simply "Lord, use me." Now we also pray, "Lord, make me usable."

Esther Undercover

Esther found herself living in a reality that must have been somewhat overwhelming to her. Imagine what it would have been like to be a young Jewish woman of simple means, suddenly deposited into the palace, with the lifestyle and expectation of Persian nobility. Every day now had a completely different and far broader perspective than she'd had before.

It probably did not take long for her to sense the national significance of her new life. Her increased territory was beginning to reveal itself in each new fresh experience. Her sphere of influence increased dramatically in a very short period of time.

But although Esther's new life was exciting, full of new things and new people, she never forgot where she came from. Esther would always be Hadassah underneath it all. Why? Because she had an unbreakable bond and deep love for her cousin Mordecai. He was her truth. He was the one person who always made her feel safe and loved: he was her home.

Esther's two different worlds caused her to live a type of dual identity. She was both the young queen and Mordecai's family. To cap off the strangeness of her identity blending, she didn't tell anyone who she really was. No one knew that Queen Esther was really Hadassah. She did this out of obedience, as Mordecai had instructed: *"Esther had not revealed her people or family, for Mordecai had charged her not to reveal it"* (Esther 2:10). *"Now Esther had not revealed her family and her people, just as Mordecai had charged her, for Esther obeyed the command of Mordecai as when she was brought up by him."* (Esther 2:20).

It is very important for us to understand the purpose of the silence that Esther chose to keep. Esther was not afraid of what people would think. She was not acting out of concern for her image or position. She kept the secret out of obedience to Mordecai.

Why would Mordecai ask her to keep her identity secret? Isn't that dishonest? Isn't it fooling the king? No! It was actually a manifestation of great wisdom. Esther's secret identity was part of a greater Kingdom strategy. God was positioning Esther for a far greater purpose that was yet to be revealed. God's timing is always perfect. He is never late. He knows the things that we don't. He sees into the areas that we don't. His plans always take every factor and variable into consideration in order to produce the best result in our lives. Mordecai was functioning by this principle—he did not want Esther to be activated in her calling until the right time had come.

Consider the biblical foundation for this:

> *For the vision is yet for an appointed time; But at the end it will speak, and it will not lie. Though it tarries, wait for it; Because it will surely come, it will not tarry.*
>
> —Habakkuk 2:3

Another translation of this passage says, *"...if it seems slow in coming, wait. It's on its way. It will come right on time"* (Habakkuk 2:3, MSG). It does us good to remember that God is true to His promises. He doesn't forget to do what He has said He will do, even though His timing does not always make sense to us. The important thing to remember is that the plan doesn't need to make sense to us. We gave up our rights in phase one. Our part now is simply to pursue the Planner and His desires. We don't need to believe in the strategy nearly as much as we need to believe in the Architect of the strategy.

Training

Notice that Esther 2:20 states that Esther was following Mordecai's instructions as she had done in her early years. It was a pattern for her to listen to and obey the one who loved her and who had taken responsibility for her life. She had grown up trusting Mordecai's wisdom. Esther's obedience in this instance was an exercise of her training; this in turn was training her for even greater levels of trust and obedience in later phases.

Keep in mind that Esther was of eligible marrying age at the time of this story. She was old enough to know her own mind and determine right and wrong—old enough to know what her heart wanted. And what she wanted, what she chose to do, was follow the wisdom and counsel of Mordecai. She chose to look on her present situation through the eyes of her foundation. She chose to trust.

Esther's decision here is an example of one who has chosen a life of surrender. She believed that Mordecai knew best and she trusted his instruction to bring about a good result in her life. God asks us to do the same. *"Trust in the Lord with all your heart, and lean not on your own understanding; In all your ways acknowledge Him, and He shall direct your paths"* (Proverbs 3:5-6).

Trust sometimes has to operate in the dark. In other words, we may not see everything clearly but past experience tells us that it is safe to trust: we trust someone or something that has already been proven trustworthy. This is training—and this was Esther's experience in her undercover season. Although she was no longer in Mordecai's home, she trusted that he was still looking after her—and he was.

Esther 2:11 states: *"And every day Mordecai paced in front of the court of the women's quarters, to learn of Esther's welfare and what was happening to her."* Mordecai continued to faithfully care for Esther and keep watch over her. She didn't always see him but she knew he was there. He never abandoned her.

Esther probably had a thousand things she wanted to ask Mordecai but she couldn't. She didn't understand the timing or reason for everything that was happening but she chose to hold onto the last thing Mordecai told her. She chose to hang on to the words and instruction of the one whom she knew loved her completely.

Deciphering the Code

Let's take another look at this passage through the perspective of the code—remember, Esther is the Church and Mordecai is Jesus.

You have been positioned by God in a place and time that may not make sense to you. You don't have access to the whole picture yet. But God has you where He does for a reason.

You may feel like you have two realities to contend with—and you do. Ecclesiastes 3:11 says that God has put eternity in our hearts. In other words, we will always have a sense of our true identity as sons and daughters of the King along with our natural, temporary reality. We are walking in a dual identity much like Esther did.

The most visible reality is that of the natural person. It is the everyday reality of family, friends, employment, finances, housing, ministry, etc. The day-to-day stuff may seem consuming at times. It is tempting to start to find your identity through position. I'm a teacher. I'm a doctor. I'm a mom, a dad, a firefighter, a pastor, a football player.

The second reality and more true identity is "Child of God." This is who you really are and this is where your life makes sense—through the eyes of relationship with Jesus.

It may feel uncomfortable and awkward to juggle two identities. There will be moments when you are tempted to quit. But it is very important that you and I remember a basic key: God is in control. He placed you where you are for His purposes. He does not want you to forget your true identity but to use it as the place from which you serve the earthly role He's asked you to fill. You are in training and there is great benefit to be experienced if you will just remain faithful.

In phase one, we learned that God will give us favour to position us for His purposes and glory. He will open doors that no one can close in order to place us where we need to be. But, after the positioning, there is often a time of waiting before the activation begins to take place.

We must trust Him and simply do the last thing He instructed. He is making a way for us where there may seem to be no way. He does not leave us undercover forever and forget us there. We might not see all the ways that He is moving but rest assured, our trust is well founded. He is watching over us.

God is not just watching over you and me, He is also watching over His word: *"Then said the Lord to me, 'You have seen well, for I am alert and active, watching over My word to perform it.'"* (Jeremiah 1:12, AMP).

God is always actively moving to fulfill His word, even when we can't see it. There are portions of time when our view may become clouded and the road ahead unclear, but we would do well to remember that *"He who promised is faithful"* (Hebrews 10:23). We don't put our expectation in the promise, but in the One who made the promise.

What kind of promise am I talking about? What kind of a word from God? I'm speaking about the very personal word of destiny that He has spoken over your life—the hope and future that He planned for you to live out.

Have you ever received a prophetic word from God for your life? Sometimes it comes by way of another person who moves in the gift of prophecy. God will use such a person to confirm the stirring that He has placed in your heart. Other times, a prophetic word comes to you directly in the way of dreams, visions or a stirring from the Holy Spirit when you are reading Scripture.

It's an awakening of a calling that has been in you for all of time. God knit you together. He wrote the book of your life. He had a plan for you that was and is good.

> Prophetic promise simply opens the eyes of your understanding to see and comprehend what has always been written on the pages of your heart.

Prophetic promise simply opens the eyes of your understanding to see and comprehend what has always been written on the pages of your heart.

But a personal promise from God does not mean instant advancement. The promise needs time to mature. Your identity will be challenged. Your faith will be exercised. It's not an easy place but it is an essential place. Though it may seem as though nothing is happening to move us toward our destiny, that is not the truth. God is always at work. But we must remember, while our timing might be more comfortable, His timing is perfect. Once again, you are in training. And your training will be tested—you will be tested.

Testing

Consider the life of Joseph for a moment, as described in Genesis chapters 37-41. Remember the dreams he had from God that indicated he was called to some form of prominence? He had visions of his brothers and parents bowing before him.

Remember also that Joseph walked in an unusual level of favour. His father favoured him over all his other brothers and even made a special coat of many colours to express that favour.

Now recall what happened to Joseph after he had the favour and a sense of destiny: he was hidden away, first as a slave and then as a prisoner in Egypt. It is interesting to note that even though Joseph was taken away from his family and made a slave, the Bible says in Genesis 39:4 that Joseph found favour. He was looking for it, and he found it. He followed the favour, and it led to him managing his master's house.

Through no fault of his own, Joseph ended up being taken from his master's house and was thrown in prison. Favour led him there: *"But the Lord was with Joseph and showed him mercy, and He gave him favor in the sight of the keeper of the prison."* (Genesis 39:21). God was actually in this. He was with Joseph and gave him favour. Joseph found and followed the favour and then God gave him even more favour. You see, the favour was positioning him. In verse 23 of that chapter we read *"the Lord was with him; and whatever he did, the Lord made it prosper"* (Genesis 39:23).

Joseph had not done anything to deserve the isolation and imprisonment. It wasn't an easy place to be. He had had a dream. He had once had a vision of greatness, but now he was an imprisoned slave. It would have been so tempting to let the dream die in this place of hiddenness.

It's exciting for us to realize is that Joseph wasn't out of God's will; he hadn't missed it. Rather, he was undercover and in training waiting for the appointed time. In the meantime, Joseph wasn't passive and still. He didn't whine, protest or give up. He chose to serve where he was, with his whole heart. He chose to operate in excellence. The Word tells us that God was with him and gave him favour. God blessed him, but didn't yet activate him. Why?

> *He sent a man before them—Joseph—who was sold as a slave. They hurt his feet with fetters, he was laid in irons. Until the time that his word came to pass, the word of the Lord tested him.*
>
> —Psalm 105:17-19

According to Psalm 105, there was something very important going on *in* Joseph along with all that was happening *to* him. He was being tested. He was developing as a man of wisdom and grace under the guidance of the Lord. He was also learning to be fully dependent on God. He was learning that everything in his life wasn't only about him, but that he was part of a bigger Kingdom, a Kingdom where God was the master of all things.

Joseph was sent ahead of his people to be part of a divine rescue that was being set in place years before it was needed. Joseph was part of a far bigger strategy than he could ever have known. It was a plan that took time and positioning. It was a time of waiting for global events to align with God's strategy. But through it all, God walked with him and gave him favour that positioned him to be in the right place at the right time for activation.

Times of testing are always about promotion. Tests are there to assure our readiness. When the time came for the Word of the Lord to be activated in his life, Joseph was prepared for it. He had been trained, tested, and he had matured while he had faithfully lived out his days undercover.

Maturing

What does all of this have to do with Esther, or with us? The experience of Joseph is very much a prototype of God's preparation program. There is always a time of preparation and maturation required before full activation.

The vision or dream is important in this season. God wants us to know that we are headed somewhere; Proverbs 29 tells us that this divine revelation of vision is vital if we are to make wise choices. But, the vision, dream or prophetic word is almost always for an appointed time that we must wait for. It needs to mature in us.

Esther had favour, she had positioning, she had a sense of destiny and she had a wise advisor who told her to stay undercover. Esther was being trained, tested, and she was maturing into her calling.

Consider what Esther went through in those first months and even years after being selected by King Ahasuerus. She was responsible to develop in a number of ways. After she was selected, she would have needed to familiarize herself with palace protocol, formal etiquette, names and positions of countless people. It would also have been vital that she have at least a basic understanding of the political and legal structures of the land. It must have been a steep learning curve. All these lessons would have been invaluable training for how she was to handle herself in the important years to come. It may have seemed like earthly training but it was really a preparation for Kingdom service.

Don't you think there must have been days that Esther wanted to cry out in frustration and fatigue? Don't you think she would have loved to hear the confirmation and comfort from someone saying they believed in her? How wonderful it would have been to be able to ask a friend to remind her of her true identity. But Esther was on her own just like Joseph was on his own. Why? Because the solitude of this undercover season trains, tests, and matures God's people like nothing else can. In this season, God has to become your lifeline—your everything.

Do you recall how the Bible records the way Mary handled herself and the prophetic happenings after Jesus was born? Do you remember what she did when the shepherds came and shared the angelic song that had been sung? "*Mary kept all these things and pondered them in her heart*" (Luke 2:19). She kept all these things to herself. She had a prophetic word from God about who her child really was. She too had found favour with God (Luke 1:30) so she could be used by God.

Mary was visited by an angelic messenger. She miraculously conceived through the power of the Holy Spirit. The heavens erupted with praise at her child's birth. Although she was walking in God's miraculous assignment, she still did not feel the need to shout out from the rooftops. She did not brag about who she was or who her son was. No, Mary simply pondered these things in her heart. She allowed the word to mature.

There is great safety in keeping some things to ourselves until the appointed time has come. It is the best way to stay undercover and allow God to do what needs to be done.

It is like a pregnancy. The first three months of a human pregnancy are the most dangerous. It is the time when a woman is most at risk of complications or miscarriage. Because of the vulnerability of these early weeks and months, most women take extra precautions to take care of themselves and nurture the development of the baby—they take no unnecessary risks.

In the spiritual realm, the development of a new spiritual dream is also at greatest risk in its early stages. We must exercise wisdom and caution. Just as the woman's body is a safe place for a baby to develop, the hidden places of God are the safe places for our destiny dreams to develop. The enemy would love nothing more than to see us be careless and put our very precious destiny seed in harm's way. The demonic spirit of abortion is on the prowl to destroy the dream before it gets a chance to reach maturity. The prophetic seed must be protected until God says it is time to come out of cover.

Another example found in the Word is the story of Moses. Exodus 2:11-15 tells the story of Moses killing two slave masters to protect the Hebrew slaves. When Moses rose up as a deliverer before his time, the very people who he was called to deliver mocked him. They did not see his actions as helpful. Moses' calling was not received nor his leadership recognized because it was not yet God's time.

I'm sure you would agree how very vital these stories are to our understanding of strategy. They provide us with valuable examples of phase two timing. They teach us what it takes to be a successful undercover agent of revolutionary change.

Esther was a young woman of simple roots who was called to do extraordinary things. As the next few years of her life unfolded, her development was remarkable. She did indeed end up being a transformational reformer of a nation but we must remember that she started by being a young woman who was willing to follow the advice of the one who loved her. She kept doing the things she'd been trained to do. She followed the favour, she embraced where it led her and, as this second phase indicates, she was willing to be an undercover operative for the Lord.

I don't know where you are at today in this journey. I hope you have a vision or prophetic word from God to hold on to. If not, I would suggest you ask for one. Ask God what He is training you for. Ask Him to reveal to you the dream that was in His heart for you the day He breathed life into your body. What are you fashioned for? What has He placed in you?

Once you know the dream, choose to stay undercover with it until the time of God's revealing. Don't concern yourself with who knows it and who doesn't. Don't allow pride to get in and cause you to broadcast it too soon. Remember, this is what the spirit of abortion is hoping you will do.

Simply be faithful. Ponder these things in your heart and carry on. Serve, learn, grow, develop and be matured by the training and testing of the Word.

God knows you. He has not forgotten you. Remember Mordecai walked past the court to check on Esther every day. God has His eye on you and He will not forget you. Simply wait on Him. Trust Him. Choose to obey out of love for Him. Be brave enough to embrace what the Psalmist said: *"But as for me, I trust in You, O Lord; I say, 'You are my God.' My times are in Your hand…"* (Psalm 31:14-15)

Prayer

Dear God, I thank you that You know who I am. I thank You for reminding me, once again, that You are in control and that You have a plan for my life. I ask You to bring assurance to my heart, even now, of the higher calling to which You are drawing me and I ask You to help me be faithful to that call. I don't want to get ahead of You and

I don't want to quit early. I declare today, Lord, that I trust Your ways and methods and that I believe my times are in Your hands. Help me to stay hidden in You until the right time, and help me to live fully in the undercover place. Refine me, O God, and do Your good work in me. I believe that because You have begun the good work, You will be faithful to complete it in me.

I am Yours!

CHAPTER VII

PHASE THREE: ACTION IN OBSCURITY

Preface

EACH ONE OF US IS VITALLY IMPORTANT IN THIS JESUS REVOLUTION. BE alert, watchful and prayerful as we move forward along this journey. God is raising up a mighty army in this hour, and we would do well to respond to His call with all seriousness and alertness.

In 2 Corinthians 2:11, the Apostle Paul reminds us that the devil is trying to take advantage of us. He reminds us that we are not unaware of his schemes. In other words, the track record of the past has shown us how our adversary operates.

One thing we know for sure, as was mentioned in the last chapter, is that the enemy tries very hard to disrupt the things of God while they are yet in their infancy. He tries to cause an abortion of destiny before it has the opportunity to come to fruition. The first few phases must be guarded from familiar attacks of the past. In this case the attack comes in the form of slumber.

Consider the first few moments of your day. The alarm rings and you roll over and hit the snooze button once or twice. It often takes a moment to remember what day it is and what you have planned for that day. You may run through a bit of the schedule in your mind to prepare yourself, and then you roll out of bed ready to face the day. But have you ever noticed how tempting that bed looks while you are still in your pajamas? Have you felt the draw to crawl back in—just for a few more minutes of rest? That pull changes once you get dressed, make the bed, and have your first cup of coffee, doesn't it? This is where the warning is for us today.

We have been awakened from our spiritual slumber. The alarm bells of the King of Glory have sounded. We recognized that although we have favour in certain areas of our life, that favour is not simply for our personal enjoyment. It is to propel us toward our mission.

We have learned that there may be a season of hiddenness to face. That hiddenness may be uncomfortable. People may misunderstand us and we may, at times, feel isolated and vulnerable. We may not be able to see how God is working at all. In this phase, we are matured, built up, disciplined and tested for service.

It is often at this point in the awakening process that the spirit of slumber attempts to whisper in our ears once again. He may say things such as: "this isn't worth it," "lots of other Christians live without this kind of extreme thinking and they seem happy," "are you really going to lose your salvation and miss heaven if you choose to live a more peaceful life?" Do any of these phrases sound familiar?

The truth is that Jesus loves us no matter what we do or how we serve Him in the Kingdom. And no, you will not lose your salvation if you choose not to be a frontline member of the awakening. But the question is honestly: how much of this is really about you and me? Isn't this whole journey about the desire of our King? Shouldn't His desires become ours as well? So what does the Word tell us He desires?

And He said to them, "Go into all the world and preach the gospel to every creature. He who believes and is baptized will be saved; but he who does not believe will be condemned."

—Mark 16:15-16

The Lord is not slack concerning His promise, as some count slackness, but is long-suffering toward us, not willing that any should perish but that all should come to repentance.
—2 Peter 3:9

"For we are God's fellow workers; you are God's field, you are God's building"(1 Corinthians 3:9). Our King has a desire for His inheritance. He sent forth labourers into the field and advised us to pray for even more labourers, because the fields are ripe for harvest. Every one of us has an assignment to fulfill, a place in the Jesus revolution.

Action in Obscurity

And now—phase three. We spoke in the last chapter about the place of hiddenness that God often calls us into as a place of undercover preparation. As we move on to phase three, we will explore a level of action that is opened to us even while we may still be hidden away in the secret place. This step is revealed to us in the last few verses of Esther chapter 2:

Now Esther had not revealed her family and her people, just as Mordecai had charged her, for Esther obeyed the command of Mordecai as when she was brought up by him. In those days, while Mordecai sat within the king's gate, two of the king's eunuchs, Bigthan and Teresh, door-keepers, became furious and sought to lay hands on King Ahasuerus. So the matter became known to Mordecai, who told Queen Esther, and Esther informed the king in Mordecai's name. And when an inquiry was made into the matter, it was confirmed, and both were hanged on a gallows; and it was written in the book of the chronicles in the presence of the king.
—Esther 2:20-23

This passage tells us so much about how God can begin to infiltrate a governmental system when He has men and women who are willing to partner with Him and obey His commands. At first glance, it may seem like a rather small action that took place, but quite honestly, it was a pivotal point in advancing the Kingdom and moving toward a national reformation.

Let's consider some of the key facts surrounding the story. Firstly, notice that Esther was functioning undercover in her position in the palace. She carried out the business of the position to which she had been called. She stayed in the palace and stayed out of the things happening outside the palace. She stayed on her assignment

Secondly, notice the position of Mordecai "within the king's gate." Mordecai now had a reason to be within the king's territory—he was checking on Esther. He was allowed to sit inside the king's gate to inquire after her, and to be kept aware of what was going on in her life. In fact, according to some interpretations of this account, it is possible that Esther had actually given Mordecai an official position. This would have granted him free access inside the king's gate at Esther's request. Now maybe this was not that big of a deal, at least not if we are simply reading the story. But, because we are analyzing it for strategic content, the little details should make much more of an impact on us.

A thorough reading of this story shows no other time when Mordecai sat within the gate prior to Esther's crowning. He did not work there. There is nowhere else in the historical account indicating that the king's gate was a normal gathering place for anyone without royal access. Mordecai was inside the king's gate simply because Esther was on assignment within the king's palace. This is huge! Remember that Mordecai is a type of Christ, Esther is a type of the Church, and the king is a type of governmental authority. So by reading the story according to these codes, we are able to understand the phenomenal truth it holds.

Deciphering the Code

Esther, representing you and me, was doing what God had assigned her to do with her life. She was faithfully serving the king while being true to the instructions of Mordecai. She wasn't making a big scene about her lot in life, or her failed dreams of the future. She wasn't throwing a temper tantrum nor was she planning her escape route. No! She was obediently living and thriving in the place she had been planted, as she awaited further instructions. She was being trained, tested and matured.

Let's think about what it means that Mordecai represents Jesus. Because Esther was in position in the palace, Mordecai had a right to come and sit within the king's gate due to his connection with her; he had been invited in. The gate represents the access to the land. Gates are the place, in both the natural and the spiritual, through which all things are allowed or disallowed access to the kingdom. Jesus is invited to come and be within the gates of our nation because we want Him there. He has access to come in because of the relationship we have with Him.

Some of you might think this understanding belittles God. You may be thinking, "Isn't God sovereign?" "Can't He go wherever He wants?" Well yes, He is and He can, but He chooses to function on Earth through relationship with us. Choosing to see through the eyes of relationship is actually honouring the mode and method through which God chose to establish His rulership on the Earth. He goes where we go; He is active where we are active. It is all about delegated authority. Recall the verses mentioned earlier in this chapter. Notice that it says He sends labourers into the harvest field. The Great Commission is a call to action to go and be Jesus' representatives on this earth. Consider the way His commission is recorded in the book of Matthew:

And Jesus… spoke to them saying, "All authority has been given to Me in heaven and on earth. Go therefore and make disciples of all the nations, baptizing them in the name of the Father and of the Son and of the Holy Spirit, teaching them to observe all things that I have commanded you; and lo, I am with you always, even to the end of the age." Amen.
—Matthew 28:18-20

We can easily see in these verses that, yes, Jesus does indeed have all authority to move here on the Earth. We can also see that He chooses to delegate that authority to us. He sends us out, and He goes with us.

This is the same concept that we see modeled in the Garden of Eden at the very beginning of humanity's tale. God was in sovereign control of the Earth, but He delegated authority for its governing and stewardship to people. Even when Adam and Eve messed up and invited sin into the world, God allowed them to do it. He gave free will to humans, and He did not take it back.

If God did not intervene and take back the reins from the first human couple, what would ever make us think that He would choose to do it in our time?

There is no indicator in the Bible that God's plans or methods have changed. He simply waits and woos us by the Holy Spirit until we come to a saving knowledge of Him. From there, it is His plan that we not only become converts but also disciples. A disciple is one who follows and learns from the teacher to the point of being identified as being like him.

Because Jesus was sent into the world to express the love of the Father, we too are sent into the world to express that love. It is an active and ongoing relationship. We provide the willing vessels and He provides the supply for all that follows. Relationship opens the gate. Our obedience and partnership creates an access point through which God can enter a situation and bring about miraculous, transformative change.

We provide the willing vessels and He
provides the supply for all that follows.

Esther on Assignment

Pressing into Esther's story a little further, we find two villains.
These two men wanted to destroy the king. We can identify
these two by their character: they were rebellious and filled
with disdain for the authority of the land. These are demonic
characteristics. They are reflective of the basic traits that Luci-
fer manifested when he rose up against God.

God is deeply committed to authority. It is His design and
He will protect it. Notice that in this case, as the ungodly attitudes rose up to challenge and to attempt to bring down authority, Mordecai intervened. The really exciting part of this is
how he intervened: he sent word to Esther and revealed the
plot to her. He didn't go straight to the king himself nor did he
just try to send word through a messenger. Mordecai chose to
use the relationship he had with Esther and the strategic position she had been placed in. He sent word into the place where
Esther had influence.

Again, following the code of the story, we find the principles of the Kingdom of God played out through Mordecai's
actions. Because Esther was in the kingdom, and because she
was in relationship with Mordecai, it created a space for him to
be within the gates of the king. From that vantage point, he was
able to thwart an attempt against the king by commissioning
Esther to carry a message.

Esther created a space for Mordecai to move. He partnered with her to make a difference and to protect the king.
Most importantly, Esther fulfilled her assignment in Mordecai's
name. Reread the account in chapter 2 verse 22. It says, *"Esther
informed the king in Mordecai's name."* That statement alone is

enough to remind us that this whole journey is not really about us as much as it is about our King and His Kingdom.

It's never about our wisdom, our creativity, our strategy or our authority. Our part in the Jesus revolution is always about revealing and honouring Him. We do what we do in His name. We are representatives of Him and our actions reflect upon Him. The actions of Esther were very strategically significant and would be understood by the unfolding of events in the weeks, months and years that followed. It was a seed of transformation planted for the future.

This action of intervention would one day, a few years and a few phases down the road, become the king's first introduction to the name of Mordecai. The kindness shown in Mordecai's actions prepared the path to ensure that the king's first impression of Mordecai would be positive. It would be clear to the king that Mordecai was respectful of the position Ahasuerus held, and that he honestly had the king's best interest at heart.

If we are ever to impact the governmental systems and structures of our nation, it must be done from a place of love. We must desire to see our nation succeed. We must honour the authorities that are in place, and we must earnestly desire what God desires for them. Acting out of rebellion and dissension falls into the same camp as the two traitors in this story. It leads to our own destruction. On the other hand, if we walk honourably and justly, God can use us to model His character. We can become a positive example of the love of Christ and we actually create an environment that makes those around us want to know more about Him.

Sowing for the Future

In Esther chapter 6 we read the next portion of this particular event, which has great merit several phases down the line. We will get into that later. For now, let's just look at the part that relates to the incident in question:

"That night the king could not sleep. So one was command-ed to bring the book of the records of the chronicles; and they were read before the king. And it was found written that Mordecai had told of Bigthan and Teresh, two of the king's eunuchs, the doorkeepers who had sought to lay hands on Ahasuerus. Then the king said, "What honor or dignity has been bestowed on Mordecai for this?" And the king's servants who attended him said, "Nothing has been done for him."

—Esther 6:1-3

To put this in the simplest terms, we could say that al-though the king did not recognize the intervention and saving power of Mordecai in the moment, there soon came a time when he did. Upon realization of Mordecai's role in saving his life, the king sought to honour him.

Sometimes obedience is about planting the seed in order to see harvest at a later time. One of the key principles of the Kingdom of God is that there is always a time to plant and a time to harvest. We sometimes need to remember that there is a long time between planting and harvesting. Often the time is longer than we would like it to be, but eventually the season of harvesting will come.

In the case of Ahasuerus, there was no immediate response, but eventually the seed that had been planted bore fruit in God's larger plan of national transformation. As it says in Zech-ariah 4:10, we should not despise the days of small beginnings. God always has far bigger things in store as we are faithful in the small things He places right in front of us.

This portion of Esther's story doesn't simply teach us about relationship, authority, access points and strategy; it also teaches us about the necessity of learning in each phase. Esther's train-ing and testing in phase two prepared her for phase three. Phase three was now training her for phase six.

Esther experienced obeying Mordecai's voice and going before the king with a message long before her life was on the line. She was given a practice run to help hone her calling. God calls us to greatness, then He cultivates and sculpts that greatness though many less-than-exciting avenues. He puts us in positions that create opportunities for us to experience the early phases of the call long before it is in full bloom.

It's like learning to swim. We teach children how to swim by first allowing them to play in the shallow end. We want them to learn to love the water. We teach them the easy moves, simple strokes that could save their lives, but would most likely not help them swim the English Channel—at least not yet. These simple strokes and techniques lay a foundation that allow them to be able to do greater things down the road. Without even realizing it, while performing these beginner moves, the child increases in fitness and stamina, and gains a confidence about their ability to stay afloat.

In this third phase of the Jesus revolution, God will cultivate His relationship with you. He will use the access you give Him to begin to develop you as an agent of the Kingdom. Because you are in relationship and you are alert to your role as an undercover agent, you will begin to start asking the right questions. You will learn to listen for instructions. And hopefully, you will learn to obey.

The things God opens your eyes to see may not seem like that big of a deal. You might not feel that your response will affect much in the big picture. Yet, it is vital that we learn to obey in this phase. We can't despise the time of small beginnings. The missions God sends you on in this phase are every bit as important in the long haul as the missions you will get down the road, and they must be handled with the same level of care. We must do everything we do as unto the Lord.

It's okay if you aren't satisfied to stay in the small places. In fact, that is a good sign since we are only on phase three of ten, but we must remember that every step matters. We can't move up if we are not faithful where we are planted today.

Have you ever heard the phrase "dress for the job you want—not the job you have"? This sentence is a comment on reaching higher. We will never advance if we only try to scrape by with the minimum effort expected of us. When we pour ourselves into the lower levels, we soon find ourselves moved into a place of greater significance. In the Kingdom, the way to rule is to serve. The way up is down. God can do great things through a heart of humility and devotion. Make a place for the King in the kingdom of this world and watch what He can do from His position at the gate!

Prayer

God, I thank you today for the places of small beginnings. I thank You that You care about those small things and You know the great things You can make out of them. Help me to be faithful to the call even when I don't understand its significance. Please help me to hear Your voice and instructions clearly, and to be quick to respond and obey.

I thank You that our relationship gives You access into all those things that concern the governing of my life. I invite You to intervene in these places. God, I ask for Your wisdom and guidance into the structures governing my life, and I ask that You would help me to carry You into those places. I believe You have a plan. I believe You want to see Your Kingdom come and Your will be done on the Earth. And God I thank You for whatever ways You might choose to do that through me. Here I am, Lord— send me.

I am Yours!

CHAPTER VIII

PHASE FOUR: MORDECAI IS IDENTIFIED

Please read Esther chapter 3 before moving on to this next phase.

As we move into Chapter 3 of the book of Esther, we find ourselves being introduced to a twist in the plot that is all too familiar. We also find ourselves being introduced to a character who is well known to us in other forms—Haman. The further into the story we go, the more we will realize that we know this man, or at least the spirit he represents. We have seen him in action so many times in history. Our spiritual eyes can easily perceive what his appearance on the scene means.

As we enter into this portion of the story and choose to read it with eyes of discernment, we are quickly reminded of the far bigger scope of this account. It readily calls to mind the times in which we now live and the realities of the current state of life in our nation:

> *After these things King Ahasuerus promoted Haman, the son of Hammedatha the Agagite, and advanced him and set his seat above all the princes who were with him. And all the king's servants who were within the king's gate bowed and paid homage to Haman, for so the king had commanded concerning him. But Mordecai would not bow or pay homage. Then the king's servants who were within*

the king's gate said to Mordecai, "Why do you transgress the king's command?"

—Esther 3:1-3

These first few verses of this chapter lay out for us the foundation for the great conflict that will be unpacked throughout the rest of the story. Haman was busy positioning himself to influence the nation. He had a public persona that was very appealing, but he also had a very different, very dark, private identity that was yet to be seen by the kingdom.

The king was in need of assistance and chose to empower Haman—the one who was destined to bring about a time of great conflict.

As this part of the story begins to unfold, we start to gain an understanding of some of the reasons why Esther needed to be assigned to a position in the seat of government. It was vital that she have a foot in the door of governmental happenings. There was a great power shift in the works and her position would become a key to future events. These first few verses also give us greater understanding of the reason why a complete Jesus revolution is the only way; halfway will never work against an enemy bent on destruction.

King Ahasuerus was a famous and powerful man who ruled over a large percentage of the civilized world in his day. He had wealth and power and absolute authority. While it is true that Ahasuerus made laws and decrees that affected the whole of his kingdom, it is also true that a kingdom of that size required an extended leadership base. There were many princes, advisors and governors who aided the king in his decision-making. They were his eyes and ears into places that he was not able to physically go. They explained to him the state of affairs in the realm, and advised him on the correct responses and actions required.

Can you imagine how helpless that would feel as a leader? Ahasuerus held great responsibility, but would have been dependent on the accuracy of the reports of his advisors in order to rule well. It would have been immensely difficult to hold absolute power while living with such a loose grasp on affairs of state. How comforting it would have been to find a personal advisor who would be loyal, trustworthy, wise and socially intuitive.

And so enters Haman. In the midst of all the pressures of rulership, Haman emerged on the scene as one the king could rely on. We discover a little later in the story that Haman was actually so respected by the king that he was invited to counsel in the inner chambers. He was given a position above the other princes of the land, which made him King Ahasuerus' right-hand man.

The problem with this? Firstly, Haman wanted his own kingdom far more than he wanted to protect the kingdom of Ahasuerus. Secondly, Haman absolutely hated the Jews.

Deciphering the Code

Let's take a moment to break this down according to the symbolic code that helps us to understand our four main characters. From that perspective, let us analyze what happened to the governmental system.

It's important for us to remember that Haman is not simply a person; he is representative of a demonic principality that wants to rule and dominate the land. His true identity will become clearer as we move through the story and view both his attitudes and actions. For now, it is sufficient to say that although King Ahasuerus found Haman's presence to be comforting and worthy of promotion, there was far more going on behind the scenes than the king realized.

The kingdom of Persia was in a time of great transition. Ahasuerus was a new king, a younger king, who would need time to earn the trust of his people. Every kingdom gets a little skittish during a season of transition.

Next, there was the very public display of ridding the kingdom of one queen and crowning another. The constants of the king's court had been altered. This kind of transition can be difficult to navigate and is greatly aided by the assistance of solid counsel. When the winds of change are blowing and everything is shifting, people often look for a calm and solid place to stand. And this is exactly what the king did.

He made a way for someone else to speak into the decisions of the land. He opened up his heart and mind to insight from someone who could never rule in his own right. He opened his nation to the demonic.

Haman in Canada

At this point in Canadian history, we too are suffering the effects of transition. The electronic age, which is marked from 1941 to the present, has aggressively and radically altered our society. Our culture has been forced to change as we have become increasingly connected with the global community. We have been technologically empowered to do more. But somehow with the advancement of "more," we are experiencing far less of quality life.

Canadians are showing signs of increased mental and physical health issues due to stress, which seems to be an unavoidable reality in this generation. We have become constantly connected online and yet somehow increasingly disconnected within our families and relationships. We are facing, for the first time, such concerns as cyber-bullying, Internet fraud and easy access pornography. Stories of abuses and reports of suicides and drug overdoses are rampant and provide abundant fodder for our minds in endless media feeds. We are one of the wealthiest nations in the world, and yet we have aggressive poverty problems due to easy credit and a rise of consumerism. Our nation is under attack.

It is obvious to even the simplest mind that we need help. It is true that not all the changes we see are bad, but they are still change. Even small change is hard to adjust to; when it comes on so many fronts it can prove to be almost debilitating.

At this point in history, Canada, along with many other nations of the world, is simply trying to navigate through the tumultuous waters. And here too enters our Haman. He comes in to advise our national leaders on the best way to interpret the signs of the times. He speaks up to help navigate through the barrage of social issues.

Haman advises our school systems on how best to advance and be progressive in our thinking. He tells our social groups and committees how to be politically correct and how best to stop any rocking of the boat. The problem is, he's in it to win it for himself. His strategy at this point is simply to gain access and begin to gain influence. He slips in because he seems safe and wise. All too soon though, we as a nation will realize that we have become part of a game we did not want to play, and we will find ourselves looking for a Saviour.

You may be wondering: how exactly we have begun to ask Haman for counsel? What proof do you have? Consider the voices that ring out in our governmental and social spheres today. Who is giving the counsel we hear broadcasted as absolute truth upon the public platforms of our nation? Do we hear the wisdom of pastors, prophets, or other godly men and women on the evening news? Do we, as a nation, seek counsel from God for wisdom to navigate the strange things we see around us?

Increasingly the sound we hear comes from the lips of scientists, psychologists, psychiatrists and social commentators. We seek legal counsel and look to popular opinion polls in order to evaluate what is normal and right. Our land is being advised by human wisdom and the counsel of the ungodly. But this will change! Take heart, a Jesus revolution is on the way.

Esther 3:3 says, *"but Mordecai would not bow or pay homage."* Imagine that. A decree came from the throne of Ahasuerus saying that Haman was the new right-hand man and should be honoured as such, but Mordecai would not bow. Now this wasn't a one-time event but rather a daily happening. Every time Haman passed, Mordecai made his stand:

> *Now it happened, when they spoke to him daily and he*
> *would not listen to them, that they told it to Haman, to*
> *see whether Mordecai's words would stand; for Mordecai*
> *had told them that he was a Jew. When Haman saw that*
> *Mordecai did not bow or pay him homage, Haman was*
> *filled with wrath.*
>
> —Esther 3:4-5

Haman had become a household name. He had gone from being an advisor to the king to being one of the most recognized people in the land. People followed him. They believed that he was worthy of recognition and honour because the king had said it was so. It became normal to bow to someone that they would never have bowed to before. The tides of popular opinion and behaviour had turned. But not for Mordecai—never for Mordecai. His truth would never change.

Mordecai chose to reveal his identity as a Jew in the middle of a national shift. He chose to reveal himself when it wasn't popular to do so. But really it wasn't so much a choice as it was a necessary action. He simply would not bow to Haman because he could not bow to him. Mordecai would not bow, even at the king's decree, because he could not bow in worship before any false god. There were also generational issues at play—we will explore these in a later chapter.

The rules that governed Mordecai's behaviour were not subject to change simply because a man had said it must be so. You see, God will never alter His Word to suit the needs and desires of people. Who He was and what He said hundreds and thousands of years ago still apply to every generation that has ever been and every generation that will ever be.

Recall the story of Daniel who would not stop praying even though the king commanded it, or Shadrach, Meshach and Abednego who refused to bow to the image of the king. They could not help but disobey the order of the earthly king because their truth was found in the King of kings.

Even more directly, we see this truth exemplified as Jesus was tempted by the devil in the wilderness:

> *Next the devil took him to the peak of a very high mountain and showed him all the kingdoms of the world and their glory. "I will give it all to you," he said, "if you will kneel down and worship me." "Get out of here, Satan," Jesus told him, "For the scriptures say, 'You must worship the Lord your God and serve only Him.'"*
>
> —Matthew 4:8-10, NLT

God will never bow to the kingdoms of this world.

God will never bow to the kingdoms of this world. He does not care about public opinion. He is not concerned with what people think they have or have not discovered to prove or disprove His existence. He is not moved when humanity decides that the pleasure they find in sin justifies any side effects they face. He does not alter the code of right and wrong based on the commonly defined standards of normal. He can't change. *"I am the Lord, and I do not change..."* (Malachi 3:6).

It is not that He won't change, or that He is unwilling to change. It is certainly not that He is power tripping or too set in His ways to change. According to His Word, He cannot change; it is not in His nature. In our world of shifting norms and redefined ideas of truth, we find Him to be the only true constant. We find that He truly is the anchor to which we must tie ourselves in order to outlast any storm.

When we analyze the details and the language of the story we can see and understand that Mordecai did not *choose* to reveal himself as much as he was *compelled* to reveal himself. He did not go out of his way to protest and fight against Haman's rule. He simply refused to participate. He did not tell others not to bow to Haman; he simply refused to do so himself.

Notice how the others by the gate confronted him about this repeatedly. They were not okay to live and let live. They wanted to know if it was acceptable that Mordecai chose to go against the grain, so they brought his behaviour to Haman's attention. They launched a complaint. This is the point in the story when Haman's true identity and his hatred begins to be revealed, and this will become even more evident as we go into the next phase.

The Lie of Grey

As much as the kingdoms and rulers of this world would like us to believe that there is room for a grey area, this is simply not so. A common area of agreement simply cannot exist; there are two eternally opposed powers at work. There is the Great I Am, King of the universe, and there is Satan, fallen angel, who is called *"the god of this age"* in 2 Corinthians 4:4. One kingdom is fully life and light; the other is fully death and darkness. There is no space in between. There is no authentic grey area.

Our society has reached a point where we are swimming in perceived grey. There is a vast void of absolute truth. There are so many opinions that it has become popular to make a space where all of them can co-exist together. There is a generally accepted decision to agree to disagree. But this concept is all smoke and mirrors; it is a false truce that doesn't really exist.

Remember the other men at the gate were uncomfortable with Mordecai's actions. They were unable to look the other way. They would not and could not be tolerant. They were compelled to force a showdown. Eventually there will always be a confrontation of kingdoms as we see exemplified through Mordecai and Haman. Look at what the Bible has to say about these so-called agreements:

Don't team up with those who are unbelievers. How can
righteousness be a partner with wickedness? How can light
live with darkness? What harmony can there be between
Christ and the devil? How can a believer be a partner with
an unbeliever?

—2 Corinthians 6:14-15, NLT

These verses don't tell believers to isolate themselves and
live separated from the world. On the contrary, we are supposed to be out and among the lost in order to be salt and light.
What the Scripture is saying, however, is that believers can't be
in covenant partnership with darkness because they belong to
two very different kingdoms. We are either identified as being
Christ's or being the devil's.

We are always and at all points in our lives identified in the
spirit by our Father. What happened to Mordecai was not recognition of his natural identity in the spirit realm, but rather a spiritual identification in the natural realm. There came a point when
the god of this age forced him to stand up and be identified. The
promotion of the false necessitated a revealing of the truth.

Again, what does this mean for us today? It means that
what God calls truth is truth. What He calls wrong is wrong.
What He says is right is right. There is no room for negotiation
or interpretation. There is no space for an evolution of truth as
we come to a higher place of enlightened understanding. God
does not change.

I know there are some advocates these days who feel many
of the guidelines we find in Scripture are cultural in nature and
therefore subject to tweaking. There are some instances when
this is valid but they are very limited and also very easily identified. These cultural instances are superficial in nature. They
are not guidelines that address absolute truth or the nature and
character of God.

For instance, there are certain behaviours and manner of
dress spoken about in the New Testament that are only spoken

of in a single place to a certain group of people. These guidelines are not repeated elsewhere in the Bible and can certainly be proven to be selective to their audience and time period.

Far more pressing are the truths and principles of God that are woven throughout the Word in multiple time frames and among many different groups of people. These things do not change and are non-negotiable. The list of non-negotiables includes such things as God's definitions of sin and the expectations He has of His people.

The Ten Commandments God gave to Moses, still applied to Paul and continue to apply to us. The expectations He had of Daniel and Peter are the same expectations that He has of us. We, as His people, should be able to easily identify what is of Him and what is not. Truth is based on who He is and what He has said. Truth will not change.

Light in the Darkness

So, what about the changes in our culture? What about our new definitions of normal? Are we supposed to get aggressive and fight about these things? The example of Mordecai tells us that he simply refused to comply. He would not have his mind changed by the most commonly accepted things. Mordecai did not try to remove the darkness at this point; he simply chose to live boldly in the light. This is how love behaves.

Being a carrier of light in the midst of the darkness is the nature of this phase in the Jesus revolution. It is not so much about the revealing of the Church at this time as it is about revealing Christ in us. The increasing spread of darkness will force a revelation of the light.

Consider the way your eyes adjust to being in a dark room. They hunt for the light, they seek it out. Any small light that may have gone previously unnoticed suddenly becomes a beacon by which we find our bearings.

This concept of light is the reason for lighthouses along the shores around the world. The shining light of the lighthouse provides a point of reference for a weary sailor trying to navigate the stormy rolling tides of the sea. It provides a marker of safety and a warning of potentially dangerous rocks below the surface.

The identification of God's people may not be comfortable, but it is necessary. It provides a constant beacon of light for a darkened world. Consider what Jesus said:

> *You are the light of the world. A city that is set on a hill cannot be hidden. Nor do they light a lamp and put it under a basket, but on a lamp stand, and it gives light to all who are in the house. Let your light so shine before men, that they may see your good works and glorify your Father in heaven.*
>
> —Matthew 5:14-16

The shining of our light leads others to glorify the Father. The purpose of being identified as different is not to embarrass you or cause you shame. On the contrary, it is about creating a platform from which the lost might be rescued and drawn to a saving knowledge of truth. The light in us, as carriers of the Saviour is a beacon of hope; we as believers cannot help but be identified with our family. We have become sons and daughters of the Most High.

Consider what the Apostle Paul has to say about it:

> *I have been crucified with Christ; it is no longer I who live, but Christ lives in me; and the life which I now live in the flesh I live by faith in the Son of God, who loved me and gave Himself for me.*
>
> —Galatians 2:20

Christ in me will always refuse to bow to the wisdom of this age and the opinion of man. Christ in me will never be moved to self-preservation at the cost of dishonouring the King.

Christ in me will always refuse to bow to the wisdom of this age and the opinion of man.

The identification *of* Jesus in this darkened age requires identification *with* Jesus. This may mean that people who liked me before may not like what I stand for when they become aware of Christ in me. People who feel they have been enlightened by the wisdom of this age may despise me for the true light I carry.

This is a good thing. The forward movement of darkness will call God's people out of hiding and cause them to be the city on a hill they were called to be. There is a necessary light that is activated as the arrogance of darkened thinking parades itself as truth. The Church cannot help but rise up when asked to bow before the lies of the enemy. Christ in us will never bow! As the Church is identified and the grey areas are removed, the next step of the Jesus revolution begins. Take heart, your King is still on His throne and He will never leave you alone.

Prayer

Dear God, I come before you today with truth burning within my heart. I have seen the winds of change in this nation and I have seen the understanding of right and wrong turned upside down. I admit that I have wondered at times how the freefall of society, as it struggles to find truth in the midst of confusion, could ever be stopped. I know in my heart that it can only be stopped by a revelation of You, and encounter with the only Truth. I believe, Lord, that You are calling me in this hour to stand before the lies of the enemy and to be identified with You. You do not bow and so, Lord, I will not bow. I ask You today to stir the resolve of my heart. Whisper Your truths to my heart. Grant me courage to stand in the presence of a kneeling crowd. Help me see clearly where common thought has deviated from Yours. I ask for wisdom to identify truth and courage to stand in it. I know the darkness reveals the light and I also know Your light chases away the darkness. I stand with You today, my God.

Jesus, I am Yours!

CHAPTER IX

PHASE FIVE: HAMAN IS REVEALED

OF ALL THE PHASES IN THE JESUS REVOLUTION, THIS ONE IS BY FAR the least enjoyable. It is the one that most aggressively assaults our senses. It pops the bubble that we sometime like to place around ourselves, and it forces us to embrace reality. It is wise to become familiar with every phase and learn the God-strategy for navigating it. Remember, wisdom brings freedom.

Knowing your enemy is of vital necessity if you are to wage war successfully so hang in there. Understanding is worth it. Remember, you are called to be a revolutionary.

Phase five is very much a part of every battle. When we know who our enemy is and where he is, we can respond in an accurate and well-measured way. We must be reminded that there can be no victory without a battle. There would be no need for a hero were there no villain, nor would we need a Saviour if we were not lost. The revelation of Haman does not create an enemy but rather it shows us that he is already present and it teaches us to cling to our Anchor.

As we finished the last phase, we saw that Mordecai had come to a place where he could no longer blend in with the crowd. The nation had listened to the instructions of the king and chose to blindly follow the call to honour Haman. They did not know him. They did not understand who he was or where he had come from. They simply did what the king said, because he was the king.

But Mordecai would not and could not bow. He could not follow the king's command. It was contrary to the command of God—and God never changes. Popular action never trumps the proper action. As you will recall, this infuriated Haman.

Popular action never trumps the proper action.

And it is here that we pick up the story:

Now it happened, when they spoke to him daily and he would not listen to them, that they told it to Haman, to see whether Mordecai's words would stand; for Mordecai had told them that he was a Jew. When Haman saw that Mordecai did not bow or pay him homage, Haman was filled with wrath. But he disdained to lay hands on Mordecai alone, for they had told him of the people of Mordecai. Instead, Haman sought to destroy all the Jews who were throughout the whole kingdom of Ahasuerus—the people of Mordecai.

—Esther 3:4-6

When Haman saw that Mordecai did not bow to him, he was overcome by his reactions. It would be a gross understatement to say that Haman was offended. It's also insufficient to say he was frustrated or aggravated. The Bible account tells us that Haman was filled with wrath. Wrath is much more than anger. In fact, its root meaning is heat, rage or poison. It means that when Haman looked at Mordecai, he was repulsed at the very sight of him. This is no small thing. There is no way to walk away from that kind of a reaction. It must be addressed. So Haman addressed it and so did Mordecai.

Haman did not consider Mordecai to be a one-of-a-kind problem. When he looked at him, Haman saw an entire race of people, a whole tribe and a kingdom. Why? Because Haman wasn't simply a man having a human reaction but rather, he was a man being influenced by the demonic realm. This was not a man who was responding to a man. It was a kingdom responding to The Kingdom.

When actions and reactions seem disproportionately large in any given situation, it is always an indicator that there is more happening spiritually under the surface. In this case, Mordecai refused to bow and Haman responded by flying into a rage toward the entire Jewish race. It is clear that this is disproportionate. That is a clue that we should look deeper; the invisible realm has just been revealed in the visible realm.

A quick overview of the third chapter of Esther shows us that Haman declared war against Mordecai and his people. He was out for blood. In an instant, we see the real reason for Haman's pursuit of governmental position. He was not involved in politics to help the king navigate through the stormy waters of change; he was about to make it stormier. He did not care about whether or not King Ahasuerus won the hearts of the people or maintained his monarchy; he was about to remove an entire people group from the kingdom.

Haman was positioned as a representative of the great adversary, and he was waiting for the strategically right moment to attack God's people. His territorial directive was to rid the land of the children of God. When Mordecai refused to bow and revealed himself as a Jew, the war was on. Though the glorification of Haman had forced action, it was Mordecai who made the first move. God always has the upper hand. This is a very important key that we will return to later on.

In order to understand the severity of Haman's wrath, we must study his next actions. They were cold, calculated and decidedly final. There would be no coming back from this kind of an assault:

Then Haman said to King Ahasuerus, "There is a certain people scattered and dispersed among the people in all the provinces of your kingdom; their laws are different from all other people's, and they do not keep the king's laws. Therefore it is not fitting for the king to let them remain. If it pleases the king, let a decree be written that they be destroyed, and I will pay ten thousand talents of silver into the hands of those who do the work, to bring it into the king's treasuries." So the king took his signet ring from his hand and gave it to Haman, the son of Hammedatha the Agagite, the enemy of the Jews. And the king said to Haman, "The money and the people are given to you, to do with them as seems good to you."

—Esther 3:8-11

The king seems to have had no grasp on what was going on behind the scenes, or else he didn't care. There was no debate or lengthy discussion. Ahasuerus did not ask for any proof of unlawful activities. He never asked who the people were, how they had gotten to Persia, which laws they disobeyed, or how Haman intended to carry out his plan. He did not even request a span of time to ponder such a drastic action. The king simply kept the whole thing at arm's length. One might even say that he was looking for plausible deniability; the less he knew, the less he could be blamed.

Whatever the reason for his lack of inquiry, it is made clear in this short exchange that Ahasuerus trusted Haman implicitly. He believed that if Haman said there was a problem, then there must be a problem. In that trust, he gave his signet ring to Haman as proof of authority. He had just given this enemy of the Jews the authority to do as he wished, with the full authority of the king. It's almost unthinkable. The actions of Haman would be fully supported and supplied in the name of the king.

Deciphering the Code

It is amazing to observe how quickly life can change once the masquerade stops. When the disguises are removed and the players are identified, the story changes almost instantly. The mask comes off and the rage starts flowing.

Notice some of the key phrases used to describe Mordecai's people. *"Their laws are different from all other people's"* and *"They don't keep the king's laws."* How familiar these phrases sound in the light of our modern age.

The laws of God are not always the same as the laws of the land. It is not that we are supposed to go against the structure that exists; in fact, God requires us to honour the laws of our authorities. The issue arises when the national laws go against God's laws.

As subjects of a higher Kingdom, we're subject to a higher law. We're supposed to obey the traffic laws, the safety laws, the tax laws and so forth. But there are certain times when our God-directed laws come up in opposition to the king's command. This will occur with increasing frequency when the demonic realm gives counsel to the nation. When this happens, Mordecai will be compelled to reveal himself. That revelation will soon force Haman out into the open as well.

In Canada, our public school systems provide a fine example of conflicting laws. Consider the fact that our kids are not supposed to pray in public school anymore. Christian teachers must present the theory of evolution without also being free to share the truth of creation. Government-funded sexual education in the classroom provides information far beyond that which God outlines as acceptable. If we think about these things for a moment we can see how kingdom laws are beginning to collide in our time every single day.

Haman Globally

There are even more astonishing examples of this conflict of laws throughout the world. Most are far more extreme than those we face here in Canada.

Consider the precious body of believers in the underground church of China. They continue to multiply in spite of their struggle or perhaps because of it. In fact, the Chinese Church is one of the fastest growing churches in the world. It is against the laws of that nation for Christians to gather and promote their faith, but the higher call of God calls them to meet together anyway. They are persecuted because of their beliefs. They are reviled because their standard for living is contrary to the government-sanctioned beliefs and is therefore considered a threat. In other words, their laws are not like those of all the other people.

I met a pastor from Pakistan a few years back whose words still grip my heart. He shared with me the story of his face-to-face encounter with persecution, his encounter with Haman. A few months prior, in an ordinary Sunday service, a group of angry men had entered the back of his church and opened fire with the guns they carried. Several members of his church were killed, and even more wounded.

That precious pastor carried with him the scars of bullets that had torn through his torso. Far deeper were the scars that he carried in his heart and mind. The memories of persecution might have caused a lesser man to quit but he pressed forward.

Should he have closed the church that day? Should he have bowed to fear? Should he have obeyed human laws or the laws of God?

I also had the privilege of meeting a woman from South-East Asia who was seeking training on evangelism in dangerous lands. Her heart was calling her home to tell her family about the love of Jesus. She shared with me that, if a person were caught evangelizing in the village she was from, it would mean death. Christian missionaries would be brought into the centre of the village, forced to kneel and be beheaded. She assured me it was true—she had seen it.

The governing laws of the village forbade evangelism but the instructions of Jesus command it. Whose law should she abide by? She had seen Haman in action, but she was not afraid. She was confident that she knew how the rest of the story would unfold. She carried an eternal hope and a sense of greater purpose.

How about us here in Canada? We don't have nearly that same level of persecution. We are not killed for our faith, or tortured to renounce Christ. Haman manifests himself in a much more tolerable way in our nation. But the spirit is the same. His hatred is the same. His plan and his purpose are the same. If the Church does not rise up, he will succeed. Edmund Burke famously said, "The only thing necessary for the triumph of evil is for good men to do nothing."

We watch public statements made on various media outlets—and we see people. Just people. Flesh and blood, just like us. We hear announcements of laws and rules and guidelines and we simply wonder how anyone could be so stupid. How could commonsense-thinking people ever come up with such insidious rules? We console ourselves by thinking it will never reach us. We are certain that such a thing could never stand up over the long run. But we must open our eyes.

It is true; the people we see and hear are ordinary men and women with families, jobs, pets and hobbies. They don't hate you. They aren't looking to destroy you. But what we do need to listen for is the scream of wrath from the evil one that can very often be heard between the lines.

There are most certainly governmental areas where the king has asked for the counsel of Haman. We are not at all talking about a war between people that is occurring; no, it is a great and timeless battle between kingdoms. The Jesus revolution is a spiritual revolution.

Most of us in this land have not had to face death in order to attend a church, but we have wondered what we would do if such was the case. You have not likely feared that you might be beheaded if you share Jesus with your loved ones, but you have considered it, haven't you? So have I. You see, our spirit sees the truth. It recognizes the potential. The conflict has not yet become life-threatening but it is most assuredly beginning to intensify. The hiding places of Haman are being revealed.

Consider one of the smallest and most obvious examples: the very simple use of the phrase "Merry Christmas." This unbelievably simple, yet God-honouring comment has been the source of a great turf war in recent years. We have become more aware as a nation that there are now many religions and belief systems co-existing in Canada. As a result, someone, somewhere along the line, decided that saying "Merry Christmas" was offensive. It was seen as pushing Christmas and in turn Christ down people's throats. Many of these other religions do not recognize or celebrate Christmas. As peace-loving Canadians, we want to be respectful. We want to make room for everybody. Someone decided that it would be far more peaceable to simply say "Happy Holidays." Let's just take the offensive word "Christ" out of there—after all, it is the polite, nice thing to do, right?

Can you hear the scream between the lines? It is the voice of Haman saying, *"Their laws are different than all the other people's."* What he is really saying is, "I don't want to give the Christians an opportunity to tell people why they celebrate Christmas, and I don't want to hear the name of Christ in any form." It may seem like a small thing but it is a telling sign within our nation.

Let's look further at what Haman had in mind. He was certainly not just trying to make Mordecai bow or make us say "happy holidays." Haman was after annihilation:

Then the king's scribes were called...and a decree was written according to all that Haman commanded—to the king's satraps, to the governors who were over each province, to the officials of all people, to every province according to its script, and to every people in their language. In the name of King Ahasuerus it was written, and sealed with the king's signet ring. And the letters were sent by couriers into all the king's provinces, to destroy, to kill, and to annihilate all the Jews, both young and old, little children and women, in one day... and to plunder their possessions.

—Esther 3:12-13

Haman's Hatred

This is one passage that is actually difficult to read through the eyes of the code. It is difficult because we don't want to believe it could be true. It is not at all comfortable to read and understand this reality. But here it is: Satan is not simply annoyed by believers; he hates us. He does not care that we are Canadian, American or Pakistani. He's at war with the One who lives within us and therefore we are his targets. He does not want to see the love of Jesus reach those who are lost. He knows we carry the answer our hurting world needs and he aims to stop us from fulfilling our mission.

Our enemy is not selective about who he hits. We see it in the phrasing of Haman's decree. He wants to see us all annihilated, young and old, male and female—everyone. Annihilate and plunder was the order given.

This is not something new. Remember, the devil's basic agenda is to steal, kill, and destroy. It's his modus operandi. It is who he has always been and what he will always want. Every principality, power and evil thing in his realm shares the same agenda.

So is God trying to scare us with this? Should we be afraid? Admittedly, it can be frightening to see the truth in print. But seeing it serves a far greater purpose, one that is well handled by our King. He knows what we are seeing. He knows what's coming and He is not at all alarmed. You see, God has a plan. The purpose of having our eyes opened to this truth is that we need to be looking to Him. We need to be awake and alert and we must be prepared to be part of His plan. See how it is recorded in Esther: *"A copy of the document was to be issued as law in every province, being published for all people, that they should be ready for that day"* (Esther 3:14).

Who should be ready? How should they prepare? Haman's intent was to prepare all the people of the land to do his dirty work for him. God's intent was quite different.

Haman wanted Mordecai's people gone. He needed the masses to come to his way of thinking in order to get the job done. But God wanted His people ready for His plan. Remember, the decree went to everybody. The Jews received the message along with everybody else.

The message that went out across the provinces sent out a shockwave of revelation. To Mordecai's people, the Jews, that shockwave signaled a mass awakening. There was no way to deny the war; there was no way to ignore the truth. Haman had been revealed and the people of Mordecai had been served notice *"that they should be ready for that day."*

What appeared to be extraordinarily bad was actually good. It was great, in fact! The truth had come to light and the people were empowered to respond. For the Jewish people of the land, there was now a clearly seen enemy. They had never been really concerned about Haman because there had been peace. The land of the Medes and Persians was full of different gods and diverse customs and there had never been a problem before.

The Jewish people had lived with a false sense of safety for a long time. They had been lulled into a spiritual slumber. The ability to agree-to-disagree had served them well—until now. You see, now they saw the underlying motives of Haman. His hatred had always been there. His plan had always been in the wings, but now they knew about it.

As we look to our great nation in this hour, it is easy to become discouraged. The enemy seems to have his hand in so many areas. We seem to have fallen so far, so fast. But God is not surprised. He is not, nor has He ever been, ignorant of the enemy's ploys. It may get worse before it gets better, but it's not the time to quit.

It may become increasingly difficult for us, as believers in Canada, to walk the walk and talk the talk. It could be that the freedoms we enjoy now in expressing our faith may be challenged to an even greater degree for a season. But according to the strategy of a Jesus revolution, Haman will only prevail for a season. We must trust God in this hour. We must cling to the Rock and know He is well able to take us through. Consider what the Word has to tell us about such times:

> *And He said to me, "My grace is sufficient for you, for My strength is made perfect in weakness." Therefore most gladly I will rather boast in my infirmities, that the power of Christ may rest upon me. Therefore I take pleasure in infirmities, in reproaches, in needs, in persecutions, in distresses, for Christ's sake. For when I am weak, then I am strong.*
>
> —2 Corinthians 12:9-10

> *And not only that, but we also glory in tribulations, knowing that tribulation produces perseverance; and perseverance, character; and character, hope.*
>
> —Romans 5:3-4

As we finish this phase, allow me to take you through one more example in the Bible that proves to us that the worse-before-better concept can be of God.

The Example of Jesus

Let's consider the early phases of the ministry of Jesus. Remember, He is the original revolutionary. It is easy to almost skip over the first thirty years of His life because the bulk of the recorded gospels tell of the days of His public ministry, death and resurrection. But there are verses and passages at the beginning of each of the four accounts that show us how Jesus went through the first five phases of revolution.

Jesus was hidden away in obscurity, a small-town boy in a small-town family. He had favour with man and with God, favour that increased with every passing year. He was trained in the hidden place. Recall the time he ran off to listen and learn in the Temple as a boy. This was a small moment of action that laid a foundation for far greater acts to come. His mother and father knew His true identity, but they kept it hidden until it was God's time to reveal the truth:

> *When all the people were baptized, it came to pass that Jesus also was baptized; and while He prayed, the heaven was opened. And the Holy Spirit descended in bodily form like a dove upon Him, and a voice came from heaven which said, "You are My beloved Son; in You I am well pleased."*
> —Luke 3: 21-22

Jesus was identified by His Father in this moment. This was a phase four moment. There could be no going back from this point. This was a public showing that He was aligned with Heaven. He was God's Son.

But then phase five came into play. Things got way worse before they got better. Revealing the identity of Jesus forced the enemy to reveal himself; that which had been skulking in the shadows was being called out by the Light: *"Then Jesus being filled with the Holy Spirit, returned from the Jordan and was led by the Spirit into the wilderness, being tempted for forty days by the devil..."* (Luke 4:1-2).

Jesus, who had done nothing wrong, who was just getting started in His ministry, who had favour from man and God—this same Jesus was led by the Holy Spirit into the wilderness. God led him into face-to-face contact with the devil. Why? It was preparation for ministry. Jesus got to hear the lies of the enemy first hand. He saw the enemy's hatred and He heard the deep desire of the evil one with every accusation. Jesus had been revealed and now Satan was revealed. It was training for the road that lay ahead of Him. It reaffirmed His identity and calling, and it showed Him the twisted nature of His adversary.

The best part comes in the verses that follow. You see the best is always yet to come. Phases one through five of the Jesus revolution are about preparation but phases six through ten are about activation. Let the following words of Luke wash over your heart and encourage you to hold the course:

Now when the devil had ended every temptation, he departed from Him until an opportune time. Then Jesus returned in the power of the Spirit to Galilee, and news of Him went out through all the surrounding region.
—Luke 4:13-14

Jesus came out of the wilderness full of the power of the Holy Spirit He was invigorated, charged up, confident and called. His world-changing ministry was launched just on the other side of his encounter with the adversary.

Church, we may be in a dark hour right now in our nation, and it may appear to be getting darker still. But the fact that we see the darkness does not mean it has prevailed. It simply means that it is time for us to rise up and take our place. There is something far greater ahead. We must stir ourselves. We must look and listen and act with discernment. We must be alert to the wrath-filled whisper of the enemy that slithers through the spaces of the public rhetoric. It is true, Haman is being revealed in this hour—but the Church is also about to be revealed. The call to action is being sounded.

Church, I implore you today, be stirred to action. Be alert to the decree of the enemy. Wake up to the agenda of Satan that is being sent out in the name of government and the dictates of political correctness. The cry of war has sounded in the heavenlies. God is on the move. He has revealed a window of time for action and we must take it. Rouse yourself from slumber and be watchful, prayerful and ready for action. The time is now!

Prayer

God, my heart is full. It is full of desire for You. It is full of calling and purpose. And Lord, it is full of the awakening to Truth. I see things around me that I don't want to see. I hear things that I don't want to hear. God, I don't want to believe that Satan has gained a foothold in our nation yet the evidence speaks the truth. But You are in control! I thank you for reminding me today to look through the eyes of discernment. I believe that what I see is subject to change at the hands of the unchangeable God of the Universe. You are awakening Your Bride to action and I am grateful to be part of the call. As my eyes are opened, I ask that You will prepare me for what lies ahead. Help me seize each day with willingness and readiness. Mould me as You desire.

I am Yours!

CHAPTER X

PHASE SIX: ESTHER IS ACTIVATED

Please read Esther chapters 4 and 5 before continuing.

THE TIME HAS COME. THIS IS THE MOMENT WE HAVE BEEN WAITING for! Brothers and sisters, fellow revolutionaries, there is indeed an answer to the ache within your heart.

Many of you have been frustrated and anguished over what you have seen and heard happening all around you. Many of you have poured out rivers tears of longing for the intervention of the King of Glory in this hour. A cry of intercession has risen from the hearts of believers across this land as Haman has been revealed before our very eyes. His presence and influence has been shocking and horrifying. So horrifying, in fact, that it has almost made us give up hope at times. Almost, but not completely—the true revolutionary can never really give up.

We know the call of God upon this land. It burns in our hearts. We believe that Canada has a prophetic destiny upon the world stage that has not yet been realized. We are certain that there is more, and we are passionate to see it come to pass. We long to behold His Kingdom come and His will done in Canada as it is in Heaven. We have watched and we have waited—until now.

I believe, with all that I am, that this is the hour of not only awakening but also the hour of activation. I believe that Canada is approaching this phase of her revolutionary journey. The reports are coming in from across the towns, cities and provinces of our nation. The intercessors are stirring. The prophets are hearing words from God. The pastors have been led to prepare for revival. The evangelists can hardly contain their excitement. There is a holy buzz in the atmosphere—for such a time as this. It is a response to the cry of Mordecai:

> *When Mordecai learned all that had happened, he tore his clothes and put on sackcloth and ashes, and went out into the midst of the city. He cried out with a loud and bitter cry. He went as far as the front of the king's gate, for no one might enter the king's gate clothed with sackcloth.*
> —Esther 4:1-2

If you close your eyes and calm your mind, your heart can hear it. It is the cry of the Spirit of God, the cry of Mordecai. It is the cry that comes forth from the very deepest parts of the soul and it shakes the atmosphere. It is the cry that changes things. It is birthed from more than simple longing, more than frustration and more than desire. It is the sound of Earth reaching Heaven and Heaven reaching through to Earth to call forth destiny. It is a frequency that somehow connects the natural with the supernatural.

Discerning the Cry

This sound has been heard before. Consider the story of Hannah in the book of 1 Samuel, the story of a woman who had been unable to bear children, and was humiliated and despised because of it. Year after year, she took the abuse but the desire never left her. She ached for more. She held in her heart the dream of bearing a child. Hannah's husband was also married to another woman, Peninnah, who had children, several of them. According to the Word, Peninnah—described as Hannah's adversary—was merciless in her contempt. It got to the point of desperation for Hannah. She needed an answer from God, and she was willing to lay her life on the line for a breakthrough:

> *So Hannah arose after they had finished eating and drinking in Shiloh...And she was in bitterness of soul, and prayed to the Lord and wept in anguish. Then she made a vow and said, "O Lord of hosts, if You will indeed look on the affliction of Your maidservant and remember me, and not forget Your maidservant, but will give Your maidservant a male child, then I will give him to the Lord all the days of his life, and no razor shall come upon his head."... So it came to pass in the process of time that Hannah conceived and bore a son, and called his name Samuel, saying, "Because I have asked for him from the Lord."*
> —1 Samuel 1:9-11, 20

Hannah was married to a man who was also in covenant with another woman, Hannah's adversary. In the beginning it was not that difficult for them all to live together; they made it work. But it was an uneasy truce that did not last long. It soon became unbearable for Hannah as Peninnah increased and she did not. Elkanah, her husband, tried to make her feel better, but could not. Hannah had reached a place of inner anguish that would not be silenced. She had reached the end of herself, and this is the place where God begins—the empty soul is one that is ready to be filled by God.

From this place of desperation, Hannah prayed and called out to God with a cry of great anguish. It is the same sound Mordecai made. It is the sound of complete surrender and complete commitment. Hannah's prayer that day included not only a petition, but also a promise. She asked for a child whom she would then dedicate fully to the Lord. She would return to God all that He gave. She was surrendering her right to mother in her own way. She simply desired that God would open the storehouse of heaven and move through her upon the earth.

It is important that we recognize and understand that Hannah's son was no ordinary boy. He was Samuel, the prophet of the Lord. Samuel's life directed the nation of Israel for decades. You see, Samuel was actually the desire of the Father's heart, birthed through the emptiness of Hannah. Hannah's cry of surrender gave birth to a prophetic promise from God. That promise, Samuel, became a conduit through which God could direct the affairs of His people. Heaven touches Earth as Earth touches Heaven through the sound of the heart cry.

Heaven touches Earth as Earth touches Heaven through the sound of the heart cry.

The sound was heard another time. It is found in the story of King David and the burning of Ziklag, found in 1 Samuel chapters 29-30. This is the story of a mighty man of war, brought to his knees in anguish. David and his men had been living as fugitives in the land of the Philistines. David's life was much like that of Esther—he was chosen by God and taken to Saul's palace. He had favour with God and with man. But the enemy rose up and David was forced into hiding. He was undercover for a season and God used this time of solitude to train and develop him. But one day, the cry came forth. As David and his men returned from the battlefield, they found their city burned to the ground and their wives and children gone: *"Then David and the people who were with him lifted up their voices and wept, until they had no more power to weep"* (1 Samuel 30:4).

Can you hear the sound? It is the sound of desperation, the sound of surrender, the sound of the heart. It is a sound that cannot come from anything but brokenness. It is a selfless sound that finds its origin in the heart-cry and even the battle-cry of the King.

The sound of weeping was soon followed by the sound of seeking. David inquired of the Lord for instructions. He asked for counsel on what to do next. It is astonishing that David and his men did not just strike out on their own in an emotional rage. But they were empty. They had been emptied of self, and they were ready to hear any command the Lord might issue.

As the story unfolds upon the pages of history, we read of a great victory. Something had been changed in that moment of brokenness, something God could use. God sent David and his men to retrieve all that was stolen and more. But it was not just about getting back what was lost; rather, it was about the activation of a new era. The cry that came from David's heart connected with the cry of *"now"* from the Father's heart.

Within weeks of the brokenness at Ziklag, there was a huge transformation within the nation. Saul and his sons were killed in battle, and David was crowned king over the nation. God had allowed Saul to be crowned king because he was the choice of the people. But when the people crowned David, they crowned the man of God's choosing. God could once again rule the land with a man who had been completely emptied of self, a man who truly desired *"Your Kingdom come, Your will be done on earth as it is in heaven"* (Matthew 6:10). The wail that was released in the emptiness of tragedy gave way to the glorious song of triumph, as God's will was done and His name lifted high in the land once again.

Allow me one more reference. You see, this sound was recorded in the pages of history another time, a very important time. It came forth from the lips of the original revolutionary. The cry was heard in the garden of Gethsemane and I have no doubt that it was also heard throughout the spirit realm as it reached through time and space to connect with the throne of God:

...And He knelt down and prayed, saying, "Father, if it is Your will, take this cup away from Me; nevertheless not My will, but Yours, be done." Then an angel appeared to Him from heaven, strengthening Him. And being in agony,

He prayed more earnestly. Then His sweat became like
great drops of blood falling down to the ground.

—Luke 22:41-44

Can you feel it? Can you hear it? Now, it is true, that we don't know what actual sound came from Jesus' lips, but we can recognize the wail of the soul. He was empty of self. He was desperate for the Father. Earthly things did not matter in this moment. It was not about food or drink, or the comforts of this world. His spirit cried out for the will of God to be done upon the earth.

Deciphering the Code

I believe that sound is unlike any other on the earth. It is not emotional. It is not planned or contrived. It is not about words or phrases. The sound comes forth when the heart cry of the Father is birthed through His people.

The sound comes forth when the heart cry of the Father is birthed through His people.

It is a resonating of the frequency of Heaven, and it lays bare the human soul. Our will, our desire, our need and our understanding are cast aside. Nothing matters nearly so much as the heart-cry of our God in this moment. The sounds of Earth are muted. The business of life stops. We lift our faces to Heaven, we tune our ears to His voice, we open our hearts to receive, the simple command—*now*!

Some of you have given voice to this cry in moments of intercession. Some feel it rumble as a roar in the depths of your belly. Still others experience it as a flood from your spirit that aches to be expressed when you worship the King. Some have not yet identified the sound, but you feel a deep churning in your inner being when you seek the heart of the Father. You know beyond all sense of reason that God has declared a "now" moment in time.

To some people this may sound completely insane. How could there be a sound that changes things? What possible good can a wail from the spirit do?

Let me say with all honesty, I can't fully explain it. I don't think any human wisdom can. You see, as it states in 1 Corinthians 1:25, even the foolishness of God is wiser than the wisdom of man. In other words, His ways don't always make sense to our natural mind. But the Spirit of God in us identifies it as Truth.

Consider the creation of the world. The Bible tells us that we have to receive that truth by faith. We don't think it, reason it or intellectually come to a place of agreement with it. It can only be received by faith. The visible world was made of the invisible world at a word from the mouth of God: *"By faith we understand that the worlds were framed by the word of God, so that the things which are seen were not made of things which are visible"* (Hebrews 11:3); *"By the word of the Lord the heavens were made, and all the host of them by the breath of His mouth"* (Psalm 33:6); *"Then God said, 'Let there be light; and there was light'"* (Genesis 1:3).

God called the entire universe into existence with a sound. It came in the form of a command, but at its core, it was sound. God wanted to create something new so He released a sound and it was so.

Doesn't it make sense that a call to action would be activated by a sound? Couldn't a national transformation be unlocked by a sound? Couldn't we be activated by such a sound?

I declare to you today that this sound is going forth across this land. The cry of *"now"* is being released! Can you hear it? Do you feel it? Does it resonate in your spirit?

With this declaration in mind, we need a solid revelation about exactly what the cry means and how it plays out in the Jesus revolution. Let's return to Esther's story to learn more:

So Esther's maids and eunuchs came and told her, and the queen was deeply distressed. Then she sent garments to clothe Mordecai and take his sackcloth away from him, but he would not accept them. Then Esther called Hathach, one of the king's eunuchs whom he had appointed to attend her, and she gave him a command concerning Mordecai, to learn why this was.

—Esther 4:4-5

Esther is Activated

The cry of Mordecai is not always pleasant. It is neither dignified nor subtle. It is not intended to be. It is meant to signal action. And in Esther's case, that is exactly what it did. But her first action was not what one might expect. Esther's first response to the cry and public display of Mordecai was distress. She didn't know how to handle it. She didn't know the cause of Mordecai's wailing but she did know that she wanted him to stop. It wasn't that she was ashamed of him, but she was uncomfortable with what he was doing. She sent down fresh clothes for him and tried to comfort him, but Mordecai would not be appeased. Esther didn't understand that Mordecai was doing what was necessary. He was releasing a heart-cry that resonated with the heart of God.

When Esther learned that Mordecai could not and would not be comforted, she began to ask the right questions. She wondered why. Why was Mordecai crying out? Why was he wearing sackcloth? Why wouldn't he be comforted?

As an answer to her inquiry, Mordecai sent back a detailed account of what was going on in the kingdom. He told her of Haman's plans toward God's people. He shared with her all the details including the personal price Haman was willing to pay to see a nation destroyed. Along with the detailed report came a specific list of instructions. The instructions indicated that the time had come for the true identity of Esther to be revealed: she was being activated.

According to the account, Mordecai commanded Esther to go before the king and plead for her people. It was neither a suggestion nor an option; Mordecai had issued a command. It was time for her to stand with her people. It was time for her to assume her true identity and become all that God had made her to be.

It had been such a long time since Esther had first come to the palace. The months had turned to years and Hadassah had been shoved to the background while Esther, her Persian identity, stood in the foreground. There had come to be somewhat of a sense of safety within the disguise. It was a false safety, a counterfeit security—the kind that might even lull a person to a sort of lethargy. But this lethargy was disturbed and shaken off by the cry of Mordecai.

The cry made room for the questions, and the questions made room for the command. This was the moment Esther had been waiting for. She was positioned for this. She had the influence to be able to say something to the right people. But fear arose, as it always does in the face of a destiny command. Fear told her that it was impossible. Fear reminded her of how small she really was in the face of such a huge adversary.

Esther wasn't the first one to face fear at the moment of activation. It is often present in such a moment—fear attacks our identity before destiny has a chance to be firmly established in our lives.

Consider what happened when Joshua was called up to lead Israel into the Promised Land. Moses had died, and it was now time for the nation to walk into the promise of God. But fear was present. It barked at the door and tried to get Joshua to back down. It tried to get him to admit defeat before the battle even began.

How do I know? Consider the words God spoke to him:

Moses my servant is dead. Now therefore, arise, go over this Jordan, you and all this people, to the land which I am giving them—the children of Israel. Every place that the sole of your foot will tread upon I have given you, as I said to Moses...No man shall be able to stand before you all the days of your life; as I was with Moses, so I will be with you. I will not leave you or forsake you. Be strong and of good courage...Only be strong and very courageous... Have I not commanded you? Be strong and of good courage; do not be afraid, nor be dismayed, for the Lord your God is with you wherever you go.

—Joshua 1:2-9

God called out Joshua and he faced fear. Mordecai called out Esther and she faced fear. God calls us out: we will face fear. But fear must bow to faith. Fear may want our attention, but you and I cannot ever bow.

Esther sent word back to Mordecai explaining why she couldn't do what he asked of her. Obviously fear caught her attention for at least a moment. She told him that the king could kill anyone who came before him without an invitation. She shared with Mordecai that she had not been called to see Ahasuerus in the past thirty days. Esther never said an outright "no" but she did give a list of compelling reasons why Mordecai's plan was impossible.

What was she really saying? She was telling Mordecai how little confidence she had in her own abilities to influence. The king hadn't wanted to see her in a month. Perhaps she had messed up. Maybe she wasn't up to his standards anymore. She doubted her own ability to turn his head when she walked in the room. She forgot favour.

One of the gateways of fear is self-consciousness: evaluating ourselves through our own eyes. When we look at what God has called us to do through the filter of our own ability, we will fear because we were never intended to fulfill the call of God on our own. The devil whispers in our ear and tells us that we are not big enough, smart enough, strong enough or influential enough to answer the call—that may be true but 1 John 4:4 states that: "...*He who is in you is greater than he who is in the world.*" We must remember, it's not about what *we* can do, but rather it is about what God can do *through* us.

God repeatedly told Joshua to be bold and courageous, and not to fear. He also told him repeatedly that He would be with him every step of the way. God did not coddle Joshua's fear. Mordecai dealt with Esther in much the same way; he did not pacify her fear. He did not send back a kind little message, saying, "You can do it honey, I believe in you." The command was straightforward and intended to result in action.

God does coddle or pacify our fear either. No, this is a war. There is no time to comfort the flesh. We cannot sit around and nurse our fears or rehearse our insufficiencies. The King of Glory has given His command and our duty is obedience. The time of questioning is long past. During the early phases of preparation, there is time for questions. There is a time for processing what is going on. But the activation phase is different. This phase requires a precision-like response to the commands and even the whispers of our King.

> *And Mordecai told them to answer Esther: "Do not think in your heart that you will escape in the king's palace any more than all the other Jews. For if you remain completely silent at this time, relief and deliverance will arise for the Jews from another place, but you and your father's house will perish."*
>
> —Esther 4:13,14

These words are pretty harsh, aren't they? They are what I call *snap-out-of-it* words. They are attention-getting and truth-bearing. They are also very telling in terms of the Jesus revolution.

Notice that the war cry has been given. Mordecai says that God will deliver His people, one way or another, with or without Esther's help. The fallout from her refusal would include the cost of her own life.

Was Mordecai giving Esther an ultimatum? Was he threatening her? Not at all. He was simply stating that God was going to do His good work with or without her. If she chose not to be part of the plan going into it, then she would be part of the casualties coming out of it. He was simply speaking the truth. He was warning her of the cost of compromise. He was declaring a principle of the Kingdom, not a threat, but an important, often stated, principle:

Therefore whoever confesses Me before men, him I will confess before My Father who is in heaven. But whoever denies Me before men, him I will also deny before My Father who is in heaven.
—Matthew 10:32-33

But Jesus said to him, "No one, having put his hand to the plow, and looking back, is fit for the kingdom of God."
—Luke 9:62

I know your works, that you are neither cold nor hot…So then because you are lukewarm, and neither cold nor hot, I will vomit you out of My mouth.
—Revelation 3:15-16

It is always all or nothing with God. He doesn't want a piece of our heart; He wants our whole heart. He doesn't want a bit of religious activity; He's looking for a life laid down as a living sacrifice. In this sold-out, all-in place, we find our new life and all we ever longed for. The request for all-in living is not a threat; it is an invitation to victory.

All of this may seem disconcerting. Fear may be trying to whisper in your ear even now. The enemy may be attempting to scare you back into the shadows of anonymity, but you have been called forth by the Light.

In order to make sure there is nothing that can be used against us, let's cover this portion of the story one more time. We want to make sure we are not missing any key pieces of understanding.

Let's talk more about the cry that Mordecai released. We must remember it is the cry of God that is released as it resonates with a sound upon the Earth. As the sound goes forth, it connects heaven and earth on a frequency that makes way for the *"now"* command from God.

Mordecai was the activator of this revolutionary cry, not Esther. Even if you are one of the people through whom the sound can be heard, you are simply uttering the sound of the Spirit as it identifies with Christ in you. Your regenerated spirit hears and acknowledges the cry. Please note: we must not think that we are capable of making the sound ourselves. We don't decide when it comes, nor can we force it to happen. The living God in us utters the cry as it connects with that which is released from the throne room of God.

Think of this cry in terms of a prophetic utterance. If a person is used by the Holy Spirit to declare a prophetic word, it is not that person's utterance. They are the vessel through which the message is delivered, but they are not the source of the message. After the word is given, the person who spoke the word then has the choice whether to listen and obey the word, or not—just like everyone else who hears the word.

Esther heard the cry of Mordecai and was uncomfortable with it at first. Once she realized that it would not stop, she took a different approach. She asked Mordecai what was going on. Mordecai responded by explaining the things that were really going on in the kingdom. He followed that up with a command.

God is doing the same with us in this hour. The sound that is being released through the land in this hour comes through men and women of God but it is His cry. For some of us, the cry that goes forth is not comfortable. We may try to mask it or ignore it, but God will not be silenced. As we humble ourselves and come before Him in prayer, we hear His voice of wisdom. We are given eyes of discernment and understanding to see what is really going on. Suddenly we see the truth. And with that revelation will come marching orders. We may not be given all the details and timelines, but we will be given our next step.

From this point on, we must be alert to the strategies of the enemy who never tires of trying to lure us into relying on our own abilities. We must remember that God has chosen us not for our ability, but our inability. He knows what He has placed in you will become mighty when empowered by Him.

We also can't underestimate the power of divine favour. God has favoured you in order to position you where He wants you for His purpose. Quite honestly, it is not about you and me at all. What a liberating truth! Fear cannot prevail when we choose to hold on by faith. We must stand firm, knowing God is able to accomplish His desire through us.

The Challenge

In Esther's activation we see the question of identity rise to the surface in full bloom. The question was posed to Esther, and it is posed to you and me today: *"...Yet who knows whether you have come to the kingdom for such a time as this?"* (Esther 4:14)

What is it that you are called to in this hour? Revolutionaries know deep within that there is more. You know you have been called for a purpose. It's not a learned truth but a gut-level knowledge. You have felt it. You know it. And as you have heard the cry of Mordecai ring throughout the land and deep into your spirit, it is time to ask: could it be that you have come to the Kingdom for such a time as this?

Prayer

O Lord, I do hear the cry of the Spirit, the cry of "now." It resonates in my heart of hearts and I know You are ready to move in this land. Father, today I ask for courage to listen to the sound, to let it move me, to let it draw me to my knees. Lord, I ask for a spirit of wisdom and revelation to teach me the truth of this moment. Show me what is real and show me where I fit in. God, I am ready for my marching orders. I rebuke the spirit of fear, in Jesus' name, the spirit that would try to make me run and hide in false peace and safety. I declare that You, O God, are far greater in me than he that is in this world. I place my trust in You. I ask you to show me, Lord: is this my time? Have I been called out for such a time as this? My ears are listening for Your command, O God.

I am Yours!

CHAPTER XI

PHASE SEVEN: ESTHER ANSWERS THE CALL

How does one even begin to articulate a response to the command of Mordecai? Is there really any phrase, word or syllable that is appropriate, other than a simple "yes"? It is the only answer that the heart will allow. But the true answer is more than a word, isn't it? The time for talking has passed and the right response is action. The activation of Esther demands movement.

You recognize this shift, don't you? It is the moment when we stop talking about doing something and we actually start moving out. Consider the last time you took a trip. You may have talked about it for years. You planned where you would go. You dreamed of what it would be like. You saved your money and purchased your supplies. You checked your passport twenty times and you reread the travel guidelines just to be sure you knew them.

Then it happened, that indescribable moment when it all suddenly became real. Maybe you felt it when you started packing. Perhaps it was not until you stood at the gate in the airport. But somewhere, somehow, quite unexpectedly, it changed. The preparation time was over, and the time of action had arrived.

Somewhere between phase six and phase seven, Esther had that moment. Reality hit and she knew that this was indeed her time to move. God had given her favour. She had been moved into the position of power that suited His design. She had endured the loneliness of the palace and the transformation from peasant to queen. She had always known in her heart that she was called to more. She believed that there was a bigger purpose for her life but she had hidden it away in her heart. God had prepared her undercover, in the secret place, for such a time as this. Suddenly she knew it, and for the first time, she truly wore her crown in the way God had intended it to be worn.

It is important for us to understand what exactly happened at this point in the transformation. We must dig in and evaluate the actions of revolution, and yes, I do mean action.

Action is a word that has to some degree lost its meaning within much of the Canadian Church. Somehow the Church of Jesus Christ, which was commissioned to go into all the world to share the Gospel, has forgotten what that commission means. We have instead embraced more of a consumer mentality. We go to conference after conference to get a touch from God. We read books and listen to endless podcasts looking for more. We run to the front of prayer lines and anointing services, looking for a touch from God through the hands of His anointed vessels.

In a way, these are good signs. They are indicators of hunger. But at some point, it is time to push ourselves away from the table and begin to use what we've received. Many of us are not in need of a fresh anointing nearly as much as we need to use the one we have already been given.

Many of us are not in need of a fresh anointing nearly as much as we need to use the one we have already been given.

What did action mean for Esther? How did she begin to move forward? How did she pick up her mantle of service? It was not in the way that many of us have been conditioned to move; her service began with humility:

Then Esther told them to reply to Mordecai: "Go, gather all the Jews who are present in Shushan, and fast for me; neither eat nor drink for three days, night or day. My maids and I will fast likewise. And so I will go to the king, which is against the law; and if I perish, I perish!"

—Esther 4:15-16

Esther's responsive action was to perform an action of humility. She began her revolutionary crusade by actively laying herself down. The fast held the key to the next step she would take.

Deciphering the Code

Let's look at the purpose of a fast. Fasting is a common practice of laying aside one's own desire and even vital necessities, such as food and water, in order to pursue God. It is a humbling of self. It was, and still is, an outward sign of an inward reality. By laying down the things of the flesh, Esther was actively saying, "God, I need You more. I can do nothing on my own apart from You, and I humble myself under Your mighty hand. You are my desire!" Consider what the Bible has to say about the practice of fasting: "*...I humbled myself with fasting...*" (Psalm 35:13);

So it was, when Ahab heard those words, that he tore his clothes and put sackcloth on his body, and fasted...And the word of the Lord came to Elijah the Tishbite, saying, "See how Ahab humbled himself before Me?..."

—1 Kings 21:27-29

Then I proclaimed a fast there at the river of Ahava, that we might humble ourselves before our God, and seek from Him the right way for us and our little ones and all our possessions.

—Ezra 8:21

Humbling of heart was what Esther was after. She needed God. Her nation needed God. It was Him or nothing. This is the place that we need to arrive at before any further action can happen.

Consider again the direction given to King Solomon: *"If My people who are called by My name will humble themselves, and pray and seek My face, and turn from their wicked ways..."* (2 Chronicles 7:14). Esther was called out by Mordecai as we saw in phase six. God had issued the cry of "now" and Esther's response was humility. She chose to partner with God and seek His ways. She sought His strategic instruction.

Why is this act of humbling so important? Why does it matter to us now? It matters because we too need to humble ourselves and seek the face of God. We too need to have fresh strategic instructions from Him.

This is a weak point in the common practices of the Church today. Not only do we continuously feed ourselves on the revelations of others, but we also feed ourselves on the strategies of others. It is common for us to look around and study what works in the lives and ministries of others so that we can duplicate it. We study why this church is growing or why that church is seeing miracles. We dissect how the group on the east end got favour with their city council, and the group on the west end experienced a breakthrough in finances.

There is nothing wrong with this search for knowledge in and of itself; the problem arises when the revelations of others are our first stop. Other people and organizations have received strategic direction from the Lord. They obeyed and it worked for them. What we should learn from them, therefore, is not the strategy they were given but rather, the lesson that they sought God for strategic instructions. We must know completely that only a God-plan will work and we will only hear it from Him. This comes through humility.

When Esther decided to respond to the call of God, she did not consult the wisdom of the land for help. There is no record of her scheming of ways to turn the king's heart. We don't read that she asked for reports on what had worked well with the king in the past. She did not seek out what had worked in any other kingdom. Her request was only of the Lord. Her first action was to come before the Lord, and humble herself and ask, "What would You like me to do next?" Humility gives birth to God's strategic instruction.

Imagine a military scenario. There is a training camp hidden away in the middle of nowhere. Soldiers have been trained here for years, brave young men and women who decided a long time ago that they wanted to fight for their country. They somehow knew they were born to be soldiers. Month after month and year after year, they prepared. Lessons on running, shooting, fighting and surviving became part of their daily routine.

One day these brave young soldiers are called into the command station to hear the news. Their unit has been called to the front. It's time for them to be who they were made to be. It's time for them to do what they had been prepared to do.

The first reaction is a form of excitement; the second is likely a sense of fear. They need to remind themselves that they are ready for this. They have been made ready. And in that moment, they decide to pack up and go.

Consider how this moving out into action would happen. They don't just grab their guns, run off the base and start fighting, do they? No, they come before their commander and ask for instructions. They know that they are part of the larger military machine. They have confidence knowing that someone who knows more than they do, has orchestrated their plan of attack. It's assumed that those making the decisions know the location, capabilities and strategies of their enemy. It's also assumed that their own capabilities are known and will be used to the best possible advantage. To be blunt, these soldiers fully obey every command they were given because their lives belong to another.

Esther did this same thing. She came before the Lord in full submission. She came in all humility to place her life in God's hands and ask for His next instructions—instructions that she would follow completely.

Humility is required because the instructions that we might receive from our Commander-in-Chief may make no sense to us at all. We must be reminded that we have placed ourselves under His headship and that therefore our own feeling or reasoning about the action becomes irrelevant.

God's Track Record

God is notorious for doing what we would term as strange or odd. He doesn't play by the rules of normalcy. Consider the instructions He has given others.

> **Joshua:** Let's start with the taking of the city of Jericho as recounted in Joshua 6. As God's people advanced out of the season of desert dwelling, and into the season of the promise, God asked them to take the city of Jericho. Joshua had a conversation with the Lord about the battle strategy He had planned. Much to Joshua's surprise, the plan included marching around the city for seven days, blowing rams' horns, and shouting. God assured him that after they did this, the shout would go forth and the great walled city would crumble and fall flat on the ground.

> **Naaman:** How about the story of the healing of Naaman, the Syrian commander, found in 2 Kings 5? He was struck with leprosy and came to the prophet Elisha to seek healing from the Lord. The instructions he received were appalling to him. He was told to go and wash himself in the Jordan River seven times to

be healed. At first these instructions were more than Naaman could handle. He felt humiliated by this instruction and it made him angry. But he was blessed to have servants with him who convinced him to humble himself and follow the instructions of the Lord. He did, and was instantly miraculously healed.

Peter: Do you recall the story of the Apostle Peter's confrontation with the tax collectors in Capernaum as told in Matthew 17? Peter came to Jesus to talk about it and Jesus came out with one of the strangest instructions ever spoken. He told Peter to go fishing. He was to grab the first fish that came up and open its mouth to retrieve a piece of money that would be enough to cover the tax for both of them.

Do you understand what God is saying to us in this phase? Our first action should be to purposefully humble ourselves and come before Him to ask for the strategic instructions. God reminds us through Esther's actions that we need to be humble in order to receive the instructions.

We may not receive an intellectually pleasing instruction. It may fly in the face of normal ideas. It won't necessarily follow any other already successful plan. It might sound unlikely, uncomfortable and maybe even downright strange. We will need to purposefully humble ourselves so that we are reminded that our lives are no longer our own. It is the only way to successfully move forward as a revolutionary.

Esther's Orders

What instructions did Esther receive? She already knew she was supposed to break the law and go before the king uninvited; Mordecai had told her that much already. There was more. There were God-designed details as to how she should go and what she should do and say when she got there. It wasn't at all what one would expect.

> *Now it happened on the third day that Esther put on her royal robes and stood in the inner court of the king's palace, across from the king's house, while the king sat on his royal throne in the royal house, facing the entrance of the house. So it was when the king saw Queen Esther standing in the court, that she found favor in his sight, and the King held out to Esther the golden scepter that was in his hand. Then Esther went near and touched the top of the scepter. And the king said to her, "What do you wish, Queen Esther? What is your request? It shall be given to you—up to half the kingdom!"*
>
> —Esther 5:1-3

Can't you just feel Esther's heart pounding in her chest? What an unbelievably nerve-wracking experience! Esther prepared herself to perfectly enhance her beauty. She would have looked good and smelled sweet. On one hand, one might think that it would have been natural for the king to respond to her favourably—what man wouldn't respond well to his beautiful wife? But we must remember that this was against the law. She could have been killed on the spot if he had been unwilling to see her—remember what had happened to the last queen?

Can you imagine how much courage it would have taken just to climb the steps up to the door of the king's palace? Can you feel her trembling as she walked across the floor toward the king? Everyone was looking. The guards, the advisors, the servants, all were waiting to see what Ahasuerus would do.

Esther lifted her gaze and her eyes met the king's and in that moment she found *favour*. There it is again, the favour. Remember, God gives us favour to position us for His purposes. We look for it and we move toward it. Esther found it with the king so she went forward and met with him face to face.

What happened next is the really astonishing part -it was likely the part of the God-plan that would have made a less humble person cry out in protest:

So Esther answered, "If it pleases the king, let the king and Haman come today to the banquet that I have prepared for him." Then the king said, "Bring Haman quickly, that he may do as Esther has said." So the king and Haman went to the banquet that Esther had prepared.

—Esther 5:4-5

We find another amazing moment when the king asked to hear Esther's request. Once again, imagine yourself in her position. What would you have said? Wouldn't it have been tempting to ask for Haman's head on a plate? Wouldn't the plea for your people be burning on your tongue? Instead, Esther showed remarkable restraint. Actually it was not restraint as much as it was humility. She was under orders. There was a larger strategy at work, and she was simply following the plan.

Do you see how very important getting the details of the God-strategy straight is?

Not only did Esther invite the king over for conversation and dinner, she also invited Haman. How revolting that must have been to her. Remember, she had seen the death warrant that he had penned. She had seen the truth of his identity. It was like inviting the devil himself to dinner! What grace it must have required. But God is in the grace business, and His grace is always enough.

At dinner that night, Esther delayed asking her request of the king. Instead, she followed the script of the God-strategy:

At the banquet of wine the king said to Esther, "What is your petition? It shall be granted you. What is your request, up to half the kingdom? It shall be done!" Then Esther answered and said, "My petition and request is this: If

> *I have found favor in the sight of the king, and if it pleases*
> *the king to grant my petition and fulfill my request, then let*
> *the king and Haman come to the banquet which I will pre-*
> *pare for them, and tomorrow I will do as the king has said."*
>   —Esther 5:6-7

As the king and the adversary ate and drank in Esther's home, she graciously served them both. She maintained her dignity and her beauty, and she did what the Lord had shown her during her fast. She was asked again by the king to share her request. Really, he was saying, "I know you didn't really just want me to come to dinner. Let's talk about what is really bothering you." How tempting! Yet Esther's actions were not dictated by the timing or wishes of the king; her steps were ordered by the Lord.

As the evening wore on, Esther continued to hold fast her resolve to do as God had instructed. She would not allow the king to tempt her into compromising the instructions of God.

Timing is essential, favour is vital and accuracy is critical. Esther was moved into position by obeying the instruction of the Lord. Think for a moment, how wise His plan was. Consider what would have happened if Esther had burst into the king's palace, uninvited, and screamed and cried before him. He would have, at best, dismissed her as being hysterical; at worst he would have ordered her death because her insolence angered him. Because of the actions she took, his curiosity was aroused. He was hanging on her every word. He wanted to hear what she had to say. God knew exactly what it would take to pique his interest and open his ears.

How did Esther find the fortitude to manage herself so well? How did she stand before the king and not quake with fear that her life would be taken from her? Where did she find the strength to sit at dinner with Haman and hold her tongue? Why was she courageous enough to attempt the impossible? It is found in the final statement she made to Mordecai:"...*And so I will go to the king, which is against the law; and if I perish, I perish!"* (Esther 4:16)

Revolutionaries, we must know that the words of Esther hold a vital key. If we perish, we perish.

Am I saying that we must be willing to die? Yes! We must know that this is not some figurative, hypothetical death we are speaking of. In actual fact, there is the possibility that the cause of Christ may cost our earthly lives. That is what is happening all over the world at this very hour.

The idea of the penalty of death for a stand of faith is unthinkable to most Canadian believers. We are familiar with the concept of emotional persecution or social ridicule and discomfort. But most of us have not allowed our minds to linger too long on the potential price of our actual lives. Why not? What are we afraid of? Doesn't our doctrine of salvation make provision for eternal life? We must evaluate these thoughts through the filter of the Word of God: *"Greater love has no one than this, to lay down one's life for his friends. You are My friends if you do whatever I command you"* (John15:13-14); *"For whoever desires to save his life will lose it, but whoever loses his life for My sake will find it"* (Matthew 16:25); *"For me, to live is Christ, and to die is gain."* (Philippians 1:21);

> *...except that the Holy Spirit testifies in every city, saying that chains and tribulations await me. But none of these things move me; nor do I count my life dear to myself, so that I may finish my race with joy, and the ministry which I received from the Lord Jesus, to testify to the gospel of the grace of God.*
>
> —Acts 20:23-24

> *For we know that if our earthly house, this tent, is destroyed, we have a building from God, a house not made with hands, eternal in the heavens...For we who are in this tent groan, being burdened, not because we want to be*

unclothed, but further clothed, that mortality may be swal-
lowed up by life...So we are always confident, knowing
that while we are at home in the body we are absent from
the Lord. We walk by faith, not by sight. We are confident,
yes, well pleased rather to be absent from the body and to
be present with the Lord.

—2 Corinthians 5:1, 4, 6-8

I know these are uncomfortable verses to read and that this is a topic we would all prefer to avoid. I also know this is a conversation we need to have. The spirit of fear would love to jump in on this and add his thoughts to the discussion. He wants you to embrace the fear because its hold will effectively hinder and even abort the movement of Esther in this hour. We need to press into this revelation and understand why Esther said what she said.

Let's take a moment to cover this in prayer before we continue: *Lord, I come before You and I thank You that Your words over me are spirit and they are life. I thank you that the laws of the Spirit of life in Christ Jesus has made me free from the law of sin and death. I take authority over the spirit of fear right now, in Jesus' mighty name. I declare that my ears are tuned to the voice of my Shepherd and I do not hear the voice of the stranger. Spirit of fear, I command you to leave now, in Jesus' name! I plead the blood of Jesus over my heart and mind and I thank you, Lord, for Your freedom, in Jesus' name!*

Conquering Fear

Fear is the number one reason the Church struggles with phase seven. Fear comes in and tells us that if we do this, something bad might happen or people might hate or ridicule you. Fear tells you to be afraid of getting fired from your job, evicted from your house or arrested. In his most aggressive and deceiving state, fear will tell you to be afraid to die.

We need to understand what is at play and why fear is a component. Fear is more than just uncertainty or a discomfort about the unknown. You see fear is half of the fear/faith equation.

Do you recall the time that Jesus calmed the storm when the disciples were being tossed on the sea in Mark chapter 4? He said *"Why are you so fearful? How is it that you have no faith?"* (Mark 4:40). 2 Timothy 1: 7 reminds us that the spirit of fear does not come from God. It has another source: the torment of the penalty of sin—death. Fear is rooted in death. It is chased out by the perfect, redemptive love of God (1 John 4:18) Fear has no place in the mind and actions of the believer.

It seems normal to fear death, but it should not be normal for a Christian. We know where we are going. We have been made alive in Christ and we have been promised that we will live with Him forever. Our eternal life has already begun. It is true that our earthly casing, the flesh, will die but our body is not who we really are. Our real identity is part of the invisible dimension.

The Apostle Paul wrote that he faced imprisonment and physical torment in every city he entered. He also said that he didn't count his life to be all that precious. If he had, he knew it would compromise his ability to finish his race with joy. He was saying that his ability to run well came from the fact that he didn't worry about holding onto his life. He was sharing with us a great truth: when we no longer fear death, we become free to truly live.

Esther's statement "If I perish, I perish" is transformative. In simple English, we would phrase it this way: "If I did, I die." If the devil can no longer use a fear of death to scare the Church into silence, then he loses his grip on the nation.

If the devil can no longer use a fear of death to scare the Church into silence, then he loses his grip on the nation.

As Esther chose to embrace the life that can never be stolen away, she became fearless. The same is true for us: fearless becomes courageous, and courageous becomes revolutionary.

Your call as a revolutionary is very personal. You may be the only person in your family who thinks like this. You may be the only person in your youth group, your Bible study group, or even your church. That's okay. Even if you feel alone in your immediate sphere, you must remember that you are part of a far bigger strategy—a revolutionary strategy.

I often think of the precision found in the design of the military forces around the world. Soldiers come in all kinds of packages and serve in many different ways. Some are pilots, some are ground soldiers, some are electronics specialists and some are covert operatives. Every division receives its own set of orders at the right time.

In this moment of history, I believe not everyone within the Body of Christ can hear the call. It is clearly heard in the hearts of some and not as clearly in others. At this step on the revolutionary journey, that is okay. Consider again the request of Esther for fasting and prayer. Esther asked those who lived with her in that city to fast and pray. There were thousands of other Jews spread throughout the land, yet she just asked for the prayers of those who were close. In other words, she was rallying those who could hear what Mordecai was saying, those who were actively in his presence and able to hear. They were asked to pray not for themselves, but for her. They were called into the bigger picture.

God is calling men and women in this hour to stand in the gap. We are being called to intercede on behalf of Esther. You are Esther, but also we, the Church in Canada, are Esther. As you fast and pray in this hour, consider well what it is you are doing. Your first action must be an action of humility.

As you come before the Lord, lay it all down before Him. Humble yourself; present yourself to Him. Come before Him not only on behalf of yourself but on behalf of the Church.

Seek His face. Be reminded of His rulership and divine strategy. Ask for ears to hear, not only for yourself, but for all throughout the Body of Christ. Ask for ears to hear the strategic instructions and courage to follow them fully. Come to Him expecting a game plan. Anticipate the next step. Ask that your fellow revolutionaries across this land would clearly hear the strategies for their own lives. Call in an army of sold-out, fully surrendered Jesus revolutionaries. And, as Mary told the men at the wedding in Cana, "*...whatever He says to you, do it*" (John 2:5).

Prayer

God, as I come before You today, I come in an act of humility. I know I need You. I humble myself under Your mighty hand and I know You will lift me up in due season. God, there is no way forward but Your way. There is no plan but Your plan. I very deliberately choose Your plan now, O God. I am listening and I am attentive to every word. I trust You with all of my heart and I choose not to rely on my own understanding. I renounce any hold of the spirit of fear in my life and I choose to walk fully by faith. My life on this Earth will not hold me back from finishing the race before me with Joy.

I pray for the body of believers across this land. I lift up my fellow revolutionaries. Give them strength, O God. Speak to their hearts. Release Your plan and Your instructions. I thank You that You give them grace and empower them for every good work, just as You give me grace and empower me. You are so good.

I am Yours!

PHASE EIGHT: HAMAN IS BROUGHT DOWN

I encourage you to read Esther chapter 6 and 7 before continuing.

PHASE EIGHT OF THE JESUS REVOLUTION BRINGS US INTO THE REALM of the miraculous. It opens the doors to national transformation that the natural mind cannot even begin to comprehend. You see, God is a God of sudden action—that is to say God's actions may seem sudden to us; to God, His actions happen right on time. We must remember that, as it is stated in Isaiah 46:10, God always knows the end from the beginning. He designs everything so that it flows seamlessly into order.

This next phase is rich with content. We must patiently and thoroughly dig through the mystery and open ourselves to the revelation it contains. If we are to fully grasp this phase, we must be prepared to let go of our limitations and remember that God is limitless. He manifests Himself in the unusual, the unthinkable, and the impossible. Our minds are used to functioning in a series of plans and structures. As revolutionaries, we must understand and accept that God may move outside of our structure. We may not always comprehend what He is doing but that is where faith must be applied. Active faith is a necessity in this part of the journey.

Unfortunately, human reasoning often struggles with the concept of the unknown. When things are unknown, we lose our ability to control or manipulate the situation. We can feel powerless when we don't know the answer to the questions of when, how, who or why. But faith is all about not knowing, at least by the natural senses. By its very definition, faith requires us to let go and trust God. Consider what the Bible says: *"Now faith is the substance of things hoped for, the evidence of things not seen"* (Hebrews 11:1).

Faith is not only unseen, it is also timeless. It doesn't exist outside of the present. The Bible says, *"Now faith..."* That's how faith works in us. Faith is now. Only now. It is not concerned with what was nor does it worry about what will be. Faith can only be active and effectual in this moment. It stands firm in this moment. It refuses all fear in this moment. Faith is obedient to the command of the Lord now.

Why a lesson on faith? Why does the concept of the unseen and the unknown matter? It matters because as soon as the transformation starts happening, our minds will try to reason it out. We will find it very tempting to look around and evaluate what has happened and what might happen in the days to come. Fear is waiting for us to give into that temptation. We must stand firm and choose faith. We must resist the impulse to try to control or understand this move of God. He will give us step-by-step instructions; our job is to simply and wholeheartedly obey.

Consider, for a moment the night after Esther's first banquet. Put yourself in Esther's place. After the king left, after Haman left, after the food was put away and the rooms put back in order, all of Esther's emotion and energy would be spent. Fatigue would have come in and washed over what had surely been a tightly disciplined mind. After risking her life before the king, carefully and wisely following God's strategy, and entertaining the demonically driven enemy of her people, Esther would have been empty. This is a tough place. It is also a vulnerable place.

What would have happened if Esther had allowed her mind to dwell on the future events of the next week, next month, or even next year? What if she had sat and re-read the order of

Haman to kill the Jews? Can you imagine the fear gate that might have been opened to her weary mind if she had allowed herself to meditate on anything beyond what God had told her to do that day?

Remember, Satan came and tempted Jesus in the wilderness at the end of His forty-day fast. In 1 Kings 18 and19, Elijah fell into an emotional breakdown immediately after he had called down fire from heaven and killed hundreds of Jezebel's priests. We must be aware that the weariness of the frontline needs to be guarded. We must watch for vulnerability in this part of the transformation process. Consider how Jesus went away to a solitary place to pray after ministry (Mark 1:35). We must be alert and firmly focused on the Lord. The weakness may come but a "now" faith will remedy it.

What does "now" faith look like? Remember, Jesus taught us to pray *"Give us this day our daily bread"* (Matthew 6:11). The manna the ancients received in the desert would only last one day. It is vital that we learn this as we move forward. We must come before the Lord daily, and we must keep our attention focused on this day—the provision for this day, the protection for this day, and the assignment for this day.

Allow me to be blunt. If we are to finish this journey we will have to put on spiritual blinders. We cannot live a revolutionary life and still be concerned about the future or the past. We cannot successfully live abandoned for Jesus, active in His revolution, and still care what other people are or are not thinking. It will be impossible to lay it all on the line if we look around to see what everybody else is doing. This revolution is a carefully orchestrated, God-designed blending of time, place and people. Keep your eyes on Him and choose to walk only by faith.

If Esther had allowed herself the luxury of observing and analyzing the scene around her, she might have lost heart to finish her mission. What her eyes would have seen in the twenty-four-hour period following the banquet would have been overwhelming, a completely bizarre mix of ups and downs. While

Esther awaited her second meeting with the king, the conflict outside her walls was escalating.

Haman and Mordecai had a series of strategic encounters that must have left the city reeling in confusion. You see, it wasn't just two men facing off, but it was two kingdoms engaged in a power struggle that would leave only one side standing. Only the eyes of faith could see and interpret correctly:

> *So Haman went out that day joyful and with a glad heart; but when Haman saw Mordecai in the King's gate, and that he did not stand or tremble before him, he was filled with indignation against Mordecai. Nevertheless Haman restrained himself and went home, and he sent and called for his friends and his wife Zeresh. Then Haman told them of his great riches, the multitude of his children, everything in which the king had promoted him, and how he had advanced him above all the officials and servants of the king. Moreover Haman said, "Besides, Queen Esther invited no one but me to come in with the king to the banquet that she prepared; and tomorrow I am again invited by her, along with the king. Yet all this avails me nothing, so long as I see Mordecai the Jew sitting at the king's gate."*
>
> —Esther 5:9-13

This section of the story is very enlightening. In it, we see a clear interpretation of the earlier tension between Haman and Mordecai. This was not a personality conflict, nor was it just a difference of opinion. This was war. Haman's words explain and reinforce the necessity of a complete revolution. Nothing less would bring a solution. Haman hated Mordecai; he could not stand the sight of him, and he would not share territory with him.

Haman started this speech to his friends and family by recounting to them all that he possessed. He named children, money, power, influence and the queen's attention as trophies of his conquest of Persia. He was a powerful and successful man by any standard—any standard except that of the spirit world. The territorial demon that motivated him could not and would not be satisfied until Mordecai and his people were wiped out of the nation. There could be no real sharing of kingdoms.

Haman's wife, Zeresh, and his friends came up with a magnificent idea, or so it seemed to Haman. They suggested that he build a gallows seventy-five feet high, and hang Mordecai on it. Notice they did not suggest that Haman simply have Mordecai knifed in a back alley or dumped in a river. The distinction is important because it shows intent. Haman did not just want Mordecai dead. He wanted him completely and utterly destroyed. It was about humiliation and domination. The plan that pleased Haman so much was all about a public display of a defeated Mordecai high above the people.

Do you recognize the symbolism in this plan? Have you spotted the reference to the crucifixion of Christ? Jesus was hated by the government of the day. They were not going to be happy until He was dead. They wanted His death to be public. They wanted to see Jesus humiliated and displayed before all the people. His body would be their trophy.

There is another interesting detail about the crucifixion that plays well into this story as well:

> *But we speak the wisdom of God in a mystery, the hidden wisdom which God ordained before the ages for our glory, which none of the rulers of this age knew; for had they known, they would not have crucified the Lord of glory.*
> —1 Corinthians 2:7-8

As much as the enemy would like to scare us into thinking he is all-powerful, all-seeing and all-knowing, he is not. According to this verse, the rulers of this age did not know the whole story. They did not know the mighty plan God was working out behind the scenes. If they had, they never would have crucified Jesus.

The cross wasn't the devil's idea—it was God's. The demonic realm watched from the outside and tried to read the signs but they were fooled. At the very moment Jesus died and the veil was torn, all hell realized they had been mistaken.

Haman implemented the same foolish plan that the ruler of the age used in Jesus' day. He fixated on Mordecai. He was not satisfied as long as Mordecai still breathed. The concept of a very public hanging seemed to appease his rage. Haman thought that his team had come up with the idea, but the Bible records the truth.

Much like the cross was God's tool for rescuing the earth, the gallows was God's tool for rescuing a nation. Again, this is discerned by the Spirit, and seen through the eyes of faith. In the natural, it appeared disastrous.

God had declared "*now*" and even Haman unwittingly complied. He moved quickly and furiously toward the confrontation. Haman's hatred was so great that he actually managed to have the gallows for Mordecai built overnight. The next morning he hurried into the king's chamber to ask the king to hang Mordecai on it.

Haman was in for a surprise. He didn't realize that the spiritual atmosphere in the palace had changed. While he had been focused on bringing Mordecai down, God had been at work behind the scenes. You see, the previous night, after the banquet, the king had been unable to rest. He had had his servants read to him from the records of the kingdom, apparently in an attempt to lull him to sleep. But remember, God had already said "*now*." The cry had gone forth, and as is so often the case with God, things had begun to be turned upside down—or perhaps I should say, right-side-up. Instead of bringing sleep, the chronicles brought forth an awakening; the king was stirred to the desire of the true King and His Kingdom.

Remember when we spoke about planting and harvest? In phase three Mordecai and Esther had planted a seed when Mordecai uncovered the plot to murder the king. Do you remember how Esther delivered the message in the name of Mordecai? Now was the time for harvest. The king was already in a bit of a heightened state. He had been waiting to see what big request Esther was going to ask for. He was intrigued by her request. I'm sure it was running through his mind as he lay sleepless in his bed that night. As God's follow-up move, He caused Ahasuerus to be awakened to Mordecai's presence. It was a positive awakening. The story of Mordecai was good, noble, righteous, and inspiring—so much so, in fact, it inspired a desire within the king to honour Mordecai, Haman's nemesis.

This story couldn't be any more fun to read at this point. I'm convinced God's sense of justice collides with His sense of humour in moments like this. Esther chapter 6 tells the almost comical tale of Haman advising the king in his chambers. Ahasuerus was looking for ideas on how to honour Mordecai. When Haman came in to the palace that morning, he missed the subtle change of atmosphere. His mind was far too full of his own ambition and scheming. The Bible tells us that Haman was convinced the honour was for him. He was cocky and prideful and getting pretty used to being favoured and honoured in the courts of the king:

> *So Haman came in, and the king asked him, "What shall be done for the man whom the king delights to honor?" Now Haman thought in his heart, "Whom would the king delight to honor more than me?"*
> —Esther 6:6

It was inconceivable to Haman that the king meant anyone but him, but God was at work!

Haman, who was after the kingdom, came up with an idea for an elaborate parade. He suggested that this person—whom he thought was himself—should be arrayed in one of the king's robes and set astride one of the king's own horses. This person should then be paraded around the king's streets by one of the king's top princes. Also, during the procession, it would be announced and declared that the king was honouring this man. It sounded like a perfect plan to someone who had his sights set on power and position.

Imagine the sick feeling that would have hit Haman when he realized that Mordecai was the man the king wanted to honour. Not only that, the king selected Haman selected to be the escort and make the declaration. This had to be the worst day of Haman's life. What he didn't yet know was that was also the last day of his life.

Let's unpack this mystery together for a moment. The enemy of Mordecai had no idea whatsoever that he had been marked for extermination. He didn't know about Mordecai's cry or that the queen was an undercover agent of the King of kings. He was not aware that the "now" order had gone forth. He didn't know that Esther had humbled herself before God, or that she had received a divine strategy that would birth a revolution in the land. Haman's lust for power and his hatred for Mordecai blinded him to some of the subtle nuances of transformation taking place within the kingdom.

Mordecai and Esther had hidden a seed—the king had now found it and Haman had been forced to broadcast it. God caught the enemy in his own trap, signaling the beginning of the end for Haman. Natural eyes could not yet see the truth of the situation, but the eyes of faith saw that a revolution was occurring at that very moment.

Imagine how this scene looked to the average person in Shushan that day:

There they were out in the marketplace, going about their daily routines. Men and women set up their shops and prepared for the day. They mulled over the happenings of the last few weeks. Life in Shushan had finally been settling into a comfortable rhythm once again. The king seemed happy, the new queen was beautiful and, Haman seemed like a pretty good guy to assist in the affairs of the palace. They didn't know much about Haman, but the king must have thought he was a good guy since he had commanded everyone to bow before him when he went past.

As they continued about their morning, they discussed among themselves the wailing that had been going on throughout the city for the past few days. They didn't know why the Jews were so bad, but Haman sure seemed to despise them. Did he know something they didn't? These were their neighbours, friends, co-workers. It was all very confusing and upsetting. So much death, so much hardship—was killing these Jews really necessary?

Suddenly the sound in the market changed as a royal procession filled through the streets. There on the king's horse sat Mordecai, the Jew! What was he doing riding the king's horse? Why had his sackcloth been replaced by the king's royal robe?

To their amazement, Haman was leading the way. He was actually shouting the praises of Mordecai and declaring that the king was honouring Mordecai. A hum rose up in the air as people chattered among themselves, attempting to sort out what was going on. Their world had spun upside down right before their very eyes.

"Should we bow?"

"Well, it is the king's procession. I suppose we should".

"Do we bow to Haman or to Mordecai?"

"Maybe both, maybe neither."

How very unsettling this whole situation was. The people looked for answers. They looked for wisdom. They looked for a safe refuge as the winds of change blew.

Underneath it all, God was at work. The nation was being alerted to a governmental shift. Questions were asked that God would soon answer. Haman may have thought the hero's parade was his idea, but God was about to take it and use it to His advantage.

Deciphering the Code

How does this translate for us today? We must look around us with the eyes of faith, and search for the unusual and the unexplainable. These are signs of the move of God showing up in some of the most unexpected ways.

Jesus is woven into the fabric of our nation. When we pull out the history books and begin to read, we find account after account of the goodness of God—His faithfulness, His provision and His plan for this land. In fact, the goodness of God is not just chronicled in the history books of our nation but it is woven throughout the fabric of global human history. It will not be ignored forever. Like the hidden story of Mordecai, the story of Jesus has been hidden away, waiting to be awakened when the time is right—at a time such as this.

One of the most unexpected places being transformed is the movie industry. It is so exciting to see the almost continuous flow of Bible-based movies and entertainment being released in this hour. For decades, the mainstream media has been diving deeper and deeper into the things of sin. They have followed the money and the money has led them to capitalize on the moral decay of our society. Marketing sin has been profitable.

Suddenly the tide has turned. It is unexpected, unusual and unexplainable but nevertheless, it is happening. One after another, films and stories of God's truth are coming out. There are movies about heaven, the life of Jesus and the truth of God's existence. There are movies about the end times and even the beginning of times. There is a buzz in the marketplace. People are wondering what is true and what isn't. Many people are picking up their Bible to see what God actually wrote.

Our society is being alerted to the presence of Mordecai, and they are being prepared for what is to come. It is as though Haman is parading Mordecai through the streets, proclaiming that he is worthy of honour. This transformation is a sign and a wonder. Revolution is happening.

Signs and wonders are being revealed in other places as well. Hard places. Devastating places. Sometimes these signs don't look much like God on the surface, but again, the eyes of faith see differently.

As the end of time draws near, the cry of anguish throughout the world is almost unbearable. There has been a vast increase in the frequency and severity of both natural and man-made disasters. People are suffering and dying from the effects of earthquakes, tornados, floods, tsunamis, hurricanes and ice storms. Even more are suffering at the hands of war, starvation and disease. These things should not surprise us. Jesus said these would be signs of the end. They are beacons indicating the times and seasons according to the timetable of God.

As the suffering occurs, it appears to glorify the power of the enemy. It is much like the self-exaltation of Haman. He felt so powerful that he couldn't imagine anyone else being honoured or paraded through the streets besides him. In our day, every terrible thing that happens—every tragedy, every loss—gives Satan a sense of satisfaction. It exalts him. Remember, the enemy's whole nature is destruction. Nothing makes him happier than widespread calamity. But, God does not see it that way. His relentless love for mankind endures. Though all may appear lost, God is at work. The tide can be turned in an instant.

The story of Mordecai, symbolizing the story of Jesus, has been tucked away for such a time as this. As people cry out in pain and frustration, they begin to look for an answer. They want to know that there is hope somewhere. In times of calamity, they remember those little Bibles they received as young people in school. The movie they saw or the documentary they viewed comes to mind. They begin to question whether or not they should bow, and if so, to whom? They pray, maybe not even knowing for certain whether God exists. In that moment of heartache, even the possibility that God is real is enough to reach toward. It is a lifeline. We need to understand that when Haman parades Mordecai through the streets, it is a signal. We must stay alert and in position. Revolution is happening.

When Haman returned home that night to prepare for the second banquet of Esther, he was dismayed. He had intended to hang Mordecai and humiliate him. Instead, he had spent the day proclaiming Mordecai's favour with the king: *"...Thus shall it be done to the man whom the king delights to honour"* (Esther 6:9). Over and over the words had rung out. *The king honours this man. The king honours this man. The king honours this man.* Oh, how that phrase must have burned in Haman's throat. How it must have pained him to form those words. You see, Haman had not simply been declaring the praises of a man—he was also prophesying the future of a nation.

As the afternoon finally reached its end, Haman covered his head and scurried home in shame. He was mortified about the affairs of the day and disgusted by how he had been forced to honour Mordecai. His wife and friends very quickly added salt to his wounds. Those who had suggested the gallows for Mordecai very hastily changed their tune. Zeresh was quick to identify the spiritual reality and prophesy Haman's demise: *"...If Mordecai, before whom you have begun to fall, is of Jewish descent, you will not prevail against him but will surely fall before him"* (Esther 6:13).

Do you hear the power of these words? *"You will not prevail against him."* Can you sense the strength and the eternal truth they contain?

Esther might not have seen it, the king might not have seen it, and even the people of the kingdom might not have seen it— but the adversary had. The revolution was already happening and the nation was being transformed.

God will never fail! He cannot be conquered by the enemy—not ever.

**God will never fail! He cannot be
conquered by the enemy—not ever.**

This is an eternal truth known by the spirit realm. When the signs were showing that God was on the move, even the enemy could not help but speak forth the truth.

Consider what the Bible tells us about the devil's battle with Almighty God—the war has been won! The winner has been decided and the loser is well informed about his future: *"Having disarmed principalities and powers, He made a public spectacle of them, triumphing over them in it"* (Colossians 2:15); *"For it is written: 'As I live, says the Lord, Every knee shall bow to Me, and every tongue shall confess to God'"* (Romans 14:11).

There is no question as to who has won the eternal war. Satan is a defeated foe. He and his horde have been served the verdict of their future torment.

The problem is that they want to take mankind with them. The battle is ugly and relentless. And though the conflict is of the spiritual realm, it manifests in the natural realm. This is why the natural world must reach into the spiritual realm for a solution. We need to understand and appropriate the strategies of Mordecai.

The final stages of Mordecai's takeover are astounding. The whole course of a nation was changed in a matter of days. But, before we step further into the unfolding of phase eight of the revolution, let's recap what had already transpired, keeping in mind that most of these events occurred over a one-week period of time. Once the revolution begins, transformation can be miraculously quick.

Recap of Events

- Haman is welcomed into the king's inner circle.
- Haman is given the honour of the king, and thereby is considered worthy of honour by the people.
- Mordecai refuses to bow to Haman.
- Haman appeals to the king.
- A decree of murder goes out.
- Mordecai cries out in the streets.
- Esther is called into action.
- Three days preparation are spent in fasting and prayer.
- Esther risks her life and goes uninvited before the king.
- Esther serves the king and Haman in her home.
- Haman builds a seventy-five-foot gallows to be seen by all.
- The king chooses to honour Mordecai.
- Haman is forced to humble himself before Mordecai and honour him publicly.
- Haman's wife prophesies his inevitable downfall.

This leads us to the next unbelievable part of the revolutionary journey. If it weren't part of documented history, it would seem almost like a fairy tale. But God moves in the impossible. We must to remember that He is limitless.

The story continues:

So the king and Haman went to dine with Queen Esther. And on the second day, at the banquet of wine, the king again said to Esther, "What is your petition, Queen Esther? It shall be granted you. And what is your request, up to half the kingdom? It shall be done!" Then Queen Esther answered and said, "If I have found favor in your sight, O king, and if it pleases the king, let my life be given me at my petition, and my people at my request. For we have been sold, my people and I, to be destroyed, to be killed, and to be annihilated. Had we been sold as male and female slaves, I would have held my tongue, although the enemy could never compensate for the king's loss." So King Ahasuerus answered and said to Queen Esther, "Who is he, and where is he, who would dare presume in his heart to do such a thing?" And Esther said, "The adversary and enemy is this wicked Haman!" So Haman was terrified before the king and queen

—Esther 7:1-6

As King Ahasuerus entered the banquet room of the queen that night, he no idea what lay before him. He didn't know what was in Esther's heart, but he knew she believed it was worth risking her life for. He was captured by her beauty and drawn in by the wisdom of her strategy. As he sat with her that night, he was ready to hear her request. His heart had been softened toward her.

Her words cut through the night with the precision of a surgeon's scalpel. Esther was not a weak, whimpering woman begging for her life. No, she was a strong, accurate warrior who moved under the anointing of God to deliver a deathblow to the domination of Haman.

There was an authority in her voice and in the words she chose. She was no longer hidden in any way. With all boldness, she picked up the mantle of leadership God had given her, and she stepped into it. Notice the words she chose: *"Let my life be given me at my petition, and my people at my request." "For we have been sold, my people and I."*

There will come a time in the life of every revolutionary when the hidden place is completely stripped away, a time when we will have to boldly step up to take our place and claim our identity. We will be called upon by the Lord to stand for the greater cause, and to identify with the larger body of believers, a time when we will truly know and understand the words of the Apostle Paul:

> *And if one member suffers, all the members suffer with it; or if one member is honored, all the members rejoice with it. Now you are the body of Christ, and members individually.*
>
> —1 Corinthians 12:26-27

Every step of the Jesus revolution draws us higher and higher in Him through an ever-greater level of surrender. In phase seven, we saw Esther faced with the challenge of being willing to risk her life as she went before the king. In phase eight, we see that God requires even more. She was called upon to stand as an intercessor on behalf of all her people. These were people she didn't know, people she might have never met nor even heard of. She was called to risk her life for strangers. Why? Because they shared the same blood line.

As we are called into this step in our own revolutionary journey, we are going to have to be willing to lay it all on the line. Not only for ourselves and our families, but also for complete strangers who are our brothers and sisters across the nation and around the world, who are suffering. We will know the poignant reality of suffering together. Also, we will celebrate the glorious wonder of rejoicing together.

As Esther stood before the king that day in all of her God-given authority, picture her splendor. She was dressed in her finest royal robes. Her hair was perfectly coiffed, make-up skillfully applied; her shoulders were back, head held high, and there was the most glorious air of confidence about her. She was not afraid in this moment. She had already laid her own life down. She beautifully and courageously stepped onto her assigned battlefield. As she did so, she found that her Commander-in-Chief, the Almighty One, had already gone before her and made a way.

The king heard the powerful words of her request and was stunned. How had someone even dared to do such a thing? How could this happen without his knowing?

In his response, we see his heart. He held no malice toward Esther. He did not hate the Jews. Clearly, he hadn't understood the deep gravity of the order he had allowed Haman to write in his name. With all sincerity, Ahasuerus asked who would do such a thing. He could not have been more stunned to hear the name "Haman" come from Esther's lips. Imagine his horror, his anger and his sense of betrayal. He had taken Haman into his confidence. He had trusted him and allowed him access into the most private parts of the kingdom. He had allowed Haman to issue decrees in his name, decrees that were supposed to protect the kingdom. Instead, this decree would tear it apart. The story tells us that Ahasuerus was so overcome with wrath that he actually had to leave the room to collect himself.

There is an important lesson for us in this portion of the story. As we study the nuances, we see great wisdom. You see, Ahasuerus was not the bad guy. He was a young king who was vulnerable in a time of transition. He had been deceived by one who sought the kingdom for himself.

Notice the way Esther conducted herself in the king's presence. She was respectful and honouring of her king. When he asked her who was to blame, she did not accuse him. She did not say, "You should know—you signed off on it." No, she put the blame where the blame belonged; she pointed to the evil residing in Haman.

In our case, we will never see our nation come to a revelation of truth if we don't behave according to the protocols of the Kingdom. We are commanded to honour God's anointed governmental leaders. We will never be in a position to affect change if we cast the blame on the wrong person.

Our government does not hate us. It does not seek to destroy Christ or His Church. Our leaders are not trying to bring about moral and social collapse across the land—but Haman is. I believe many people in positions of power have been led astray by the lies of Haman. They have aligned themselves with the wrong advisors, and in so doing, have signed decrees and made laws that are orchestrated by the prince of darkness himself. We must refuse the opportunity to judge them, criticize them, spurn them or accuse them.

It can be so tempting, at times, to look at our school boards, our city councilors, our provincial and national government leaders and be disappointed, frustrated or angry with them, but we must remember that our fight is not with flesh and blood: *"For we do not wrestle against flesh and blood, but against principalities, against powers, against the rulers of the darkness of this age, against spiritual hosts of wickedness in the heavenly places"* (Ephesians 6:12).

We are not called to war on a natural level. Our job as Jesus revolutionaries is to follow the call of God, take ownership of the position of influence He gives us, and shine a light into the lies of darkness. God will do the rest.

When Esther made her bold request, the Bible tells us that Haman was terrified. The prince of darkness knows when the light has been shone on him. It is interesting to see that Haman, who had once gloried in the honour of men bowing before him, suddenly cast himself on Esther's mercy. The description records Haman as being terrified before the king and queen, so much so that he fell across the queen's couch and begged for his life.

When the king came back into the room, after calming himself, and saw Haman sprawled across Esther's couch begging, he was enraged again. It appeared to the king that Haman was attacking the queen. Little did he know how far he was from the truth. Haman's days of attacking were over. He simply hoped that Esther would be naive enough to spare his life.

Once again I remind you, this is war. We cannot settle for any less than Haman's execution. If Esther had spared him, it would have been just a matter of time before he rose to power again. The demonic realm may act contrite, it may feign humility and remorse but it is a lie. Satan never feels bad about destruction; he is only ever sorry to have been caught. Let's pick up the story once again:

> ... *Then the king said, "Will he also assault the queen while I am in the house?" As the word left the king's mouth, they covered Haman's face. Now Harbonah, one of the eunuchs, said to the king, "Look! The gallows, fifty cubits high, which Haman made for Mordecai, who spoke good on the king's behalf, is standing at the house of Haman." Then the king said, "Hang him on it!" So they hanged Haman on the gallows that he had prepared for Mordecai. Then the king's wrath subsided.*
>
> —Esther 7:8-10

Revolutionary, can you sense the magnitude of this moment? Do you recognize what just happened? It is not simply about saving Esther's life. It is not just about saving Esther's people. The far bigger victory is that Haman is removed from power in the nation. His voice is silenced forever and his manipulation and devious counsel are put to an end.

Are you catching what I'm saying? Right here, in this moment of the revolutionary journey, the scope increases once again—Esther's personal call has now impacted an entire nation.

Remember the first steps of the journey where Esther was focused on herself, her role in the kingdom, and her ability to perform her duties at the palace. Next, she served Mordecai and delivered the message of the assassination attempt in Mordecai's name; it was about her and Mordecai. Then she was called up to serve on behalf of more than herself and Mordecai; she was commissioned to stand up for the lives of the Jews. In so doing, God positioned her to intercede on behalf of the whole nation. He used her to birth a solution to a national dilemma. He removed Haman from the entire political system and created a void that would soon be filled by a representative of the Lord.

We may have started this journey with nothing more than a sense of personal calling. As we have travelled along through the steps, we have grown in a sense of responsibility for our families and our friends. Further stages have revealed the compassion of God for all of His Body, and a corporate call to stand for the freedoms of all believers: a call to stand for what is right. But bigger still, when we stand for justice and righteousness for the body of believers, God awakens us to more. We suddenly see those who are being manipulated by the evil one. We see the lies and deceptions that have been paraded as truth, and we feel moved for those who have been lied to. God gives us His heart for the masses who have bowed before Haman simply because of an order from the king. We begin to see the lost as just that, lost. Our eyes are opened to the real source of the darkness, and we are compelled to spread the light.

The wisdom of God is astounding. If, at phase one, God had asked us to take on a national devil like Haman, and affect a governmental shift in the land, we would have run away in fear. "It's too great a work," we would have said. "I'm not able," "I have no influence," "I don't care about the whole nation." But God knows us well. He understands our limits and He gently guides us down the paths of faith, and flies with us over the valleys of the unknown. And if we are obedient, if we keep our eyes on Him, and if we will walk one step at a time, we will win. We will stand as Esther did, watching through the night as Haman is disgraced and dragged through the streets, then is destroyed by his own device. God was not concerned when Haman built the gallows. He knew what it would really be used for. He allowed Haman to continue on and lay his own trap.

We must allow our minds to grasp this truth. Faith alone will take us where we need to go. We don't need to work out every eventuality in our minds. We don't need to be able to sort out every detail. We don't have to see the big picture. We simply need to obey as we fix our gaze on the One who does. As we do, we can declare with confidence: *"And we know that all things* work together for good to those who love God, to those who are the called according to His purpose" (Romans 8:28).

Prayer

God, as I study this passage I am amazed by You. I can barely comprehend Your wisdom and might. I can see that You hold the big picture, and that You are the Master Designer of Your great work. Help me to trust You. Help me to walk by faith and not by sight. Lord, as I am obedient to You, cause me to be in the right place at the right time for Your purpose. Help me be bold enough to pick up my mantle and fulfill my mission. God, today I ask You to give me a capacity for this nation, a heart to stand and declare freedom to this land. I say today, Lord, that where I am weak, I know You make me strong. Where I am simple, You make me wise. And where I am powerless, Your great power works through me. Use me for Your glory.
I am Yours!

PHASE NINE: THE CURSE IS REVERSED

The next portion of our study of Esther is absolutely full of not only phenomenal historical detail, but also revolutionary strategy. Please Read Esther Chapters 8 and 9 before continuing.

IS YOUR HEART BURNING LIKE MINE IS AS THE REVELATION TAKES ROOT? Can you sense the victory of Christ in this story? Do you have faith for Canada to see her Haman destroyed? Do you also feel the call to even higher places than this?

There is always more in God. I don't know about you, but I want all that there is. I think every revolutionary does. We've become addicted to the presence of God; as is only fitting when we've discovered an active relationship with Him. We are reliant on Him in every day for everything. Our destiny is found only in God's design.

Our destiny is found only in God's design.

The sense of longing for more is indeed of God. We feel it because our mission is not yet finished. There is a compulsion, an anointing, to press higher because that is exactly what is required. It is important to note that there are still three more chapters in the book of Esther to be explored. The story is far from over and there is much more to learn.

The Follow-Through

Haman's death was an end and it was also a beginning. It marked the end of his direct influence with the king and the beginning of a national activation. Haman's death demanded follow-through on a far larger scale than we have previously seen in this book. It would require more than just Esther and Mordecai; it would require the cooperation of the government. Beyond governmental cooperation, full transformation would have to be taken to the streets; it would impact everybody.

We could compare this next part of the revolution to be like the birth of a baby, with national transformation being the baby. There are nine months of preparation and one day of delivery, followed by approximately eighteen years of raising and nurturing that child.

We also see this principle in action through the experience of marriage. Young people meet one another, develop a relationship, learn and grow together, become engaged and finally get married. But anyone who is married knows that although the wedding celebration may seem to be the climax, it is far from the end. Once the wedding is over, the marriage begins. The marriage is the good part. It is the active fulfillment of the dream once held by a single man or woman.

But raising a child or living out a marriage is not always easy. It takes commitment. It takes effort. It means taking responsibility for the choices and promises of the past, and daily fulfilling them in a way that honours the Lord.

Much like the birth of a child or a wedding ceremony, the death of Haman was a marker of change. It was not the end goal, but rather the first step of many to achieving the goal. In this case that goal was national transformation. The story needed to be completed with the same fervor and zeal as it had in the beginning, and perhaps even more so.

As we continue on in the phases of the Jesus revolution, we must consciously choose to walk out the win. We must endeavour to finish what God started in us, and in our nation. We must choose to live out the fullness of God's plan and bring it to a place of completion. We must consciously choose to live out the dream of God's heart.

As we step into this phase, we must be alert and ready for action. A new season has been birthed and now we must be in position to see that it is raised and developed properly. Remember, the real act of transformation has only just begun.

In sports such as baseball, golf, or tennis, training for the perfect swing includes instruction on follow-through. Follow-through is the action that happens in the moments after the ball is struck. When the follow-through isn't given its due attention, or when the player is simply focused on striking the ball, much of the power is lost. A good follow-through will increase the distance the ball will travel and the accuracy of its flight.

Our follow-through in this moment of revolution is vital as well. We must make sure that the effects of Haman's death are felt far and wide. The sting of the deathblow must land accurately in the heart of evil. We must do our part to make sure that the victory we've seen does not become a victory won in vain. Revolutionaries, we must hold the course and commit to the follow-through.

Do you recall the story of Vashti being banished by the king? It was the marker of the beginning of Esther's story. The kingdom was in transition and the king was unsure of himself, unwilling to make decisions without assistance. All of the upheaval and upset in the kingdom created a fantastic opening for Haman to make his entrance. As time went on, he increased in influence to the point that he was above all the other princes.

This would have meant that not only did the king listen to his counsel, so too did the national court. Haman had been instrumental in the shaping a nation and its laws.

Recounting this makes us realize that although Haman's execution was a great victory in the spirit, it also had great impact on the political scene. His death would have created a large vacuum in the operations and decision-making of the realm. Haman had been visible, powerful and influential. His absence would have left a void that must be filled. It was vital that he be replaced immediately. Consider what Jesus had to say about movement in the spiritual realm:

When an unclean spirit goes out of a man, he goes through dry places, seeking rest, and finds none. Then he says, "I will return to my house from which I came." And when he comes, he finds it empty, swept, and put in order. Then he goes and takes with him seven other spirits more wicked than himself, and they enter and dwell there; and the last state of that man is worse than the first. So shall it also be with this wicked generation.
—Matthew 12:43-45

I can almost hear your wheels spinning. "Now wait a minute, are you trying to say that things are going to get worse? Should we have just left Haman alone?" Not at all. The point is that the demonic realm will capitalize on any vulnerability that it can find. The cleaning of the house is not the end of the story. And if we don't finish the mission, then the enemy will finish it for us. I am saying that it has never been more important for us to keep moving. Listen to your heart: the beat of the marching drum that you hear is the beating of the heart of God, a heart of love for a nation.

Filling the Void

God is not caught off guard by this void. He is neither scrambling to find and answer nor shaking His head in confusion. He's been waiting for this. It is His master plan that is unfolding. God has already made provision for the forward movement of the Church at this phase of the revolution. He has created an atmosphere by which Mordecai may enter the national arena at the invitation of the king. This phase marks the shift from the awakening of the Church to the awakening of the nation. Watch the shift that happened in the palace that night:

> *On that day King Ahasuerus gave Queen Esther the house of Haman, the enemy of the Jews. And Mordecai came before the king, for Esther had told how he was related to her. So the king took off his signet ring, which he had taken from Haman, and gave it to Mordecai; and Esther appointed Mordecai over the house of Haman.*
> —Esther 8:1-2

The king gave the house of Haman to Esther as his follow-through move. Haman's entire estate was put in the hands of Esther to do with as she pleased. That means that every place he held power, everything he had owned or laid claim to was now hers to do with as she pleased. This was a massive responsibility. Accurate stewardship in this moment would have far-reaching results.

Esther was not equipped to handle the house of Haman all by herself. Yet, even though she was suddenly in over her head with this transfer of authority, she did not refuse it. She did not pause for even a moment of conversation with the king to discuss her inability. She did not ask the king what she should do with it; she knew what was required. You see, while Esther knew she was incapable of such a large role, she also knew one who was more than capable. Esther called in Mordecai to handle it on her behalf. She invited him to fill the void. Esther took on the challenge because she knew Mordecai would be the one doing the work. She used a very important God-principle: *"You are of God, little children, and have overcome them, because He who is in you is greater than he who is in the world"* (1 John 4:4);

> *And these signs will follow those who believe: in My name they will cast out demons; they will speak with new tongues; they will take up serpents; and if they drink anything deadly, it will by no means hurt them; they will lay hands on the sick, and they will recover.*
>
> —Mark 16:17-18

We must come to the same realization that Esther did—we can't do this alone! We are never capable of doing those things that God tells us to do on our own. We will never be big enough, strong enough or educated enough to deal with the house of Haman. But Mordecai is—Jesus is! We are able to do what we do and go where we go with all boldness because we have surrendered it all to Jesus. *"It is no longer I who lives, but Christ lives in me"* (Galatians 2:20). He is big enough. He is strong enough. He is wise enough. And as we go in His name, the power of darkness is subdued before us. When we are given the opportunity to deal with the house of Haman, we go forward boldly, knowing that Christ in us can handle it. He is the victorious one.

The next part of this phase is where it begins to get really exciting on a national scale. Esther had dealt with Haman. She had been given responsibility over his house and had placed it under the authority of Mordecai. Esther had come to a place of some personal victory and closure but she was not yet finished. It was time for the king to meet Mordecai. It's not enough that he was affiliated through Esther—the king needed to have an encounter with Mordecai himself.

Esther brought Mordecai into the palace and introduced him to the king, face to face. She explained how she was related to Mordecai. She told the king her story; one might say she shared with him her testimony. The Scripture, in Revelation 12:11, tells us that we overcome by the Blood of the Lamb and by the word of our testimony. Esther's conversation with the king and her introduction of Mordecai was about far more than a polite resolution to an ugly night—it was about overcoming.

The words used to describe this exchange are very familiar to believers. We know and understand what she did. She fulfilled more than an assignment; she fulfilled the Great Commission. The king had been devastated, betrayed and used. He was broken, angry and humiliated. Esther stepped into that brokenness and offered him hope; she offered Mordecai.

Imagine how the introduction would have gone. Maybe something like this: *"Oh my king, how can I begin to thank you for hearing my petition and listening to my plea for help? I know you feel betrayed. You have been lied to and manipulated by someone you thought you knew. I'm sure you are wondering who can be trusted after something like this.*

"I know a man who can be trusted, my king. Let me tell you about the one who is so dear to my heart, the one who has given his life for mine. Mordecai. I know you have never met him, but I am sure his name is familiar to you.

"Mordecai is my family. When I was an orphan he took me in and gave of himself to raise me, protect me, and teach me right from wrong. He told me how to behave here in the palace and he has been watching over me every day since I've been here. He is my wise counselor and he is my closest friend. I owe him my very life.

"My king, you owe him your life as well, do you remember? Mordecai is the man who intercepted the assassination attempt on your life. In fact, you honoured him just this afternoon.

"I would like to introduce you to Mordecai. I promise you, he can be trusted. He will give you good counsel. He will never lie to you, or trick you. In fact, my king, Mordecai loves you and desires

to see you succeed. He believes that you have a good future before you. He has hope for you."

As Esther finished with her introduction of Mordecai, the king took off his signet ring and gave it to Mordecai. He gave him the power and the authority to rule in Haman's stead. Ahasuerus chose to partner with Mordecai.

This sounds a lot like a conversion experience to me. The king's heart was turned from Haman to Mordecai. The signet ring was taken from Haman and given to Mordecai. Ahasuerus put his life and his kingdom into Mordecai's hands.

Consider what would have happened if Esther hadn't kept moving. What if she had believed that Haman's death was the end of the story? How would the story be different if she had allowed the stress of the day to overtake her? What if she had simply fallen into bed to sleep off her exhaustion? What if the void had been left open? But she didn't and it wasn't. Esther boldly and wisely stepped into the space that had been vacated and shared her heart with the king. She shared Mordecai.

Revolutionaries, we must realize that when we see Haman fall, it is not yet time to pause to celebrate. We cannot take a break to count our blessings. No, we must seize the opportunity. We must be ready to give a reason for the hope that we have, as we are instructed in 1 Peter 3:15. We must be bold enough to share Jesus with the lost, especially on a governmental level, as soon as the opportunity presents itself.

Lots of people struggle with the idea of witnessing to the powerful. They wonder how they could possibly minister to the emptiness of soul that is hidden by the façade of plenty. It is for certain that even the rich and powerful have such an emptiness. And it is true that while Haman is pacifying the flesh, that emptiness is often disguised.

But, there comes a time when the heart of even the very powerful and the very rich is laid bare, a moment when neither power nor money can ease the pain. It could come through the betrayal of a friend, the loss of a loved one or even just the pressures of life. That betrayal, pain, or pressure can actually create on opening for the Gospel. God waits for that opening; He anticipates it with such love and compassion. He has prepared you to walk into that opening on His behalf. He knows you don't have the answers to fix the situation. He knows you cannot mend the heart. God simply expects you to introduce the lost to Jesus. He will take it from there.

When powerful people come to Jesus, powerful things start happening. Powerful things are required to fulfill the next requirements of this phase. There is a rebuilding and restructuring that can only be sanctioned by positions of authority.

Esther had seen the fall of Haman and had introduced the king to Mordecai, but her work still was not finished. She had to be willing to step into the unresolved business that needed tending. Her heart still burned for more.

Esther was acutely aware of the damage Haman had done, and the death warrant for all the Jews that was still in effect. She knew there had to be a royal intervention of some kind. Esther appealed to the king once again. She couldn't just walk away and hope that he would figure it out. She knew that the king had a great deal on his mind, and it was possible that if she didn't stick with it, the day of the decree would still come. There had to be follow-through. It was worth it to put her life on the line one more time:

Now Esther spoke again to the king, fell down at his feet, and implored him with tears to counteract the evil of Haman the Agagite, and the scheme which he had devised against the Jews. And the king held out the golden scepter toward Esther. So Esther arose and stood before the king, and said, "If it pleases the king, and if I have found favor in his sight and the thing seems right to the king and I am pleasing in his eyes, let it be written to revoke the letters devised by Haman..."

—Esther 8:3-7

But even the king did not know how to undo the wrongs of Haman. This evil advisor had led Ahasuerus down a path with consequences that seemed unavoidable. He was aware that some action was required, but the laws of the land limited him. The order had been signed by his own hand, a fact that was impossible to ignore. The king's decree could not be reversed; it would require a wise and carefully orchestrated counter-measure—a counter-measure that could only be drafted by the hand and wisdom of Mordecai.

As Esther brought her petition to the king, he responded by delegating authority back to her and Mordecai:

> *"You yourselves write a decree concerning the Jews, as you please, in the king's name, and seal it with the king's signet ring; for whatever is written in the king's name and sealed with the king's signet ring no one can revoke."*
>
> —Esther 8:8

Sometimes the damage the enemy has done will take time to repair. This is especially true in the area of governmental realities. Laws cannot be overturned overnight. Policies must be appealed and re-appealed. There are committees and sub-committees that must pass almost every decision that affects our society. In addition to the laws and policies are referendums and government appointments that can only happen at certain times, in certain ways. The key to remember is that, if God has been given legal access by the governmental structures of the land, He will write the laws. He will move in wisdom to see His desire come to pass.

I believe a major key here is the heart condition of government officials. The king will give Mordecai access to pen the laws and decrees, but only if he knows Mordecai. We must pray for the salvation of our government officials. We must care about the condition of their hearts:

Therefore I exhort first of all that supplications, prayers, intercessions, and giving of thanks be made for all men, for kings and all who are in authority, that we may lead a quiet and peaceable life in all godliness and reverence. For this is good and acceptable in the sight of God our Savior, who desires all men to be saved and to come to the knowledge of the truth.

—1 Timothy 2:1-4

We should listen to and learn from the admonition of Paul to young Timothy in this passage. Notice that he didn't instruct him to pray for a peaceable life. He was not instructed to intercede for freedom to live in godliness. No, Paul instructed Timothy to pray for the government, to pray for the salvation of those in authority. Freedom is a natural by-product of a government that is ruled by Christ. A broken nation is not the sign of a government problem; it is the symptom of the absence of God. It is a lack-of-Jesus problem.

Freedom is a natural by-product of a government that is ruled by Christ.

Esther did not work against the governmental structure; rather, she influenced within it. The godly priority on her heart propelled her to action and caused her to dare, once again, to go uninvited before the king. Her presence brought the right issues to the forefront. We must be committed to advocate for the issues that are on God's heart too. We must be willing to put ourselves on the line—go to meetings, sit on boards, join committees and accept government positions. At the very least, dare I say, we must vote!

Esther was able to petition the king because she had a voice. Within the democratic system of Canada, our voice is heard by our vote. It is heard through our letters, emails, and phone calls.

It is heard as we get involved in the things that are happening in our cities and nation. It is heard as we, Esther, dare to continue to put ourselves before the king.

For quite some time the Church has stepped back from political issues. Many have felt that our nation seems hopeless and too far gone. Many within the Church have given up on our government and have relinquished all hope for transformation. This cannot continue. If we are to see true transformation, we must be willing to care again. We must be willing to introduce the king to Mordecai. This is our hope. In the eyes of God, we are never too far gone. His presence changes everything.

As soon as Mordecai was invited in to the situation, he got to work. He already had a plan. He was prepared for the commission of the king. He met with the king's scribes in the palace and drafted a new decree that would remedy the king's decree. He wrote a new law that would effectively reverse the curse:

> ...to every province, in its own script... and to the Jews in their own script and language. And he wrote in the name of King Ahasuerus, sealed it with the king's signet ring, and sent letters by couriers on horseback, riding on royal horses bred from swift steeds. By these letters the king permitted the Jews who were in every city to gather together and protect their lives - to destroy, kill, and annihilate all the forces of any people or province that would assault them, both little children and women, and to plunder their possessions...
> —Esther 8:9-12

Mordecai's decree did not put the Jews on the attack; it simply allowed them to defend themselves. The phrasing of the document displayed the delicate but firm hand of true nobility. It did not cause the Jews to look like whiners nor savages. It was quite simply a declaration of life. The wishes of the King of Kings were ordered and decreed by Mordecai at the request of the natural king. His desire had finally aligned with God's desire and his seal gave permission for God's will to be fulfilled.

Do you see how subtle and glorious a Jesus revolution can be? The Jews were not sent out on a rampage against the rest of the kingdom. They did not storm the gates of the palace and lay waste to the seat of government. There was not even a hint of rebellion. Their Jesus revolution was a subtle wooing of the hearts of men by a loving God. It was a binding and casting down of demonic strongholds, which led to a national, governmental shift by gracious and peaceful means. God caused the king to want to change. He helped him find his way to truth.

The Word tells us that on that day, Mordecai left the king's palace dressed in royal robes. He was wearing blue and white and had on an outer garment of linen and purple. He wore a golden crown upon his head. Everyone could see that Mordecai was now ruling in the nation. *"And the city of Shushan rejoiced and was glad"* (Esther 8:15). There was a celebration in the streets because Mordecai had taken his rightful place.

A rebellion will not bring about joy and gladness, but a Jesus revolution will. Why? Because Jesus has come to lavish on us His perfect love, and lead us into abundant life. The city and provinces may not have known the details of the past days and months, but they knew how to recognize a good thing when they saw it. They knew that the king had found some sort of peace and they knew that it would trickle down to them.

Everyone is looking for hope. When Jesus is invited into a nation, hope comes:

> …*On the day that the enemies of the Jews had hoped to overpower them, the opposite occurred, in that the Jews themselves overpowered those who hated them…And no one could withstand them because fear of them fell upon all people. And all the officials of the provinces, the satraps, the governors, and all those doing the king's work, helped the Jews, because the fear of Mordecai fell upon them. For*

Mordecai was great in the king's palace, and his fame spread throughout all the provinces; for this man Mordecai became increasingly prominent.

—Esther 9:1-4

Oh, how my spirit leaps when I read the words "*the opposite occurred.*" In other words, the curse was reversed. This is a documented governmental-level miracle. It is a moment in history when a nation's destiny was turned and aligned with the will of God because of an encounter with Jesus.

It is important to remember; though there was victory, it was a victory that had to be won. I said it was a gracious and peaceful revolution and that it was. But not all peace is easily attained. Sometimes it is about peace-making; sometimes peace must be laid hold of by force: "*Blessed are the peacemakers, For they shall be called sons of God*" (Matthew 5:9); "*And from the days of John the Baptist until now the kingdom of heaven suffers violence, and the violent take it by force*" (Matthew 11:12).

The order of Mordecai's decree was defensive in nature. It ordered the Jews to protect themselves against the attack of the enemy. They were not called to be peacekeepers, but rather peacemakers. Haman's decree launched a violent attack; Mordecai's decree countered with a forceful, definitive and godly response. Every victory is the result of a battle—it can be no other way.

This battle is to be faced and overcome. The remnant of Haman's house was still an enemy of the Jews. They hated Mordecai and his people with the same hatred that Haman had carried. Why? Because even though the territorial principality was cut off, the demonic force of his realm still existed in the land. They still knew the Jews carried truth and a life that they despised.

It's exciting to see that even though there was a battle, it was an easy win. The enemy absolutely could not stand against the forces of Mordecai. All of the king's officials stood with Mordecai. They had bought into his truth and made it their own. They had aligned themselves with him and stood to fight for him. It says "*Mordecai became increasingly prominent*"— his fame spread throughout the land. In Esther 8:17 we read, "*Then many of the people of the land became Jews, because the fear of the Jews fell upon them.*" In other words, the fear of God spread across the land. This occurred even before they went into battle. The nation was being changed from the inside out—by choice. This is a description of national transformation.

There *is* hope. There is hope for our children, hope for our families and hope for our nation. As we prepare ourselves for the final phase, let's take a moment to allow that hope to rise up in our hearts. Revolutionaries, I admonish you: "*...Position yourselves, stand still and see the salvation of the Lord, who is with you...*" (2 Chronicles 20:17).

Prayer

God, I come before You today, full of hope. I know You can do the impossible in this land. I know You have Canada in Your heart, and I know that Your plans for her are good. I pray for the leaders and officials of this land today, oh, Lord. I pray that they would meet You. God, I pray for divine appointments across this land where men and women who love You would have an opportunity to share that love. I ask for boldness for each one of us to share the Gospel. Not just with the hurting in the highways and byways, but also with the lost and hurting in positions of power and influence. God, I see that they need You, too. Encounter them. Teach them Your ways. Lead them in truth. Grant them Your wisdom. Jesus we welcome You in this land. Show us how to fight, how to stand, and how to repair the mess that the enemy has left behind him. Today I ask, Father, heal our land.

You are good, and once again I declare,
I am Yours!

CHAPTER XIV

PHASE TEN: FINISH THE MISSION

THIS IS IT; WE HAVE FINALLY COME TO THE FINAL PHASE OUTLINED FOR us in the book of Esther. It has been a phenomenal journey covering a vast array of emotions, actions, regulations, declarations and transformations—all through the strategy of revolution. We have watched and learned as the course of a nation was turned around and the King of kings was invited to rule.

As we finished phase nine, we saw a nation that was willing to fight for right. We saw a people who were moved by the fear of the Lord, and a government who freely welcomed God to take His rightful place. The people rejoiced, the curse was reversed, and a new season of Kingdom rule began.

What could possibly be left to do? What role might Esther have to play?

This final phase is all about complete closure. In fact phase ten may very well be the most important one of all. Why? Because it is the reset phase. If phase ten is not completed properly, it will very quickly reset to phase one for generations yet to come.

We pick up the story after the day of war. There had been a huge victory and according to the report delivered to King Ahasuerus, the enemies of Mordecai were defeated. It would appear that the conflict was over and the danger to Mordecai's people was eliminated. But appearances can be deceiving. Remember, our adversary is the master of deception.

Interestingly, the king did not go to Mordecai to see what he wanted to do from there. He sensed there needed to be further follow-through, so he went back to Esther to see what she desired to do.

Revolutionaries, we need to catch this; it is important. Remember, Esther is the access point. She was chosen as a conduit of the Lord, and a catalyst for change. God waits to be invited into the situations on earth. It is an expression of His delegated authority and a manifestation of the gift of free will.

As the king approached Esther to ask her wishes, we see that there is one more thing she needs to see accomplished. Her response and her request may not seem necessary. Certainly it does not seem like the request of a beauty queen. But as we learned long ago, Esther is far more than a beauty queen—she is a warrior for the King of Glory!

And the king said to Queen Esther, "The Jews have killed and destroyed five hundred men in Shushan the citadel, and the ten sons of Haman. What have they done in the rest of the king's provinces? Now, what is your petition? It shall be granted to you. Or what is your further request? It shall be done." Then Esther said, "If it pleases the king, let it be granted to the Jews who are in Shushan to do it again tomorrow according to today's decree, and let Haman's ten sons be hanged on the gallows."
—Esther 9: 12-14

At the end of a long day of fighting and great victory, Esther's request was that the same action be taken again the next day. When she heard the report that Haman's ten sons had been killed, she was not satisfied. Esther wanted to have their bodies hanged on the gallows and put on display for all to see. What bloodthirsty words! What a fine example of overkill—or was it?

We are about to see that Esther was driven by a call far greater than her own. Her request was motivated by a command much older than she. She was compelled to complete a mission that had begun six hundred years before. But let's not get ahead of ourselves; every detail of this final phase matters.

The king honoured Esther's request and sent out a decree to repeat the next day what had been done that day. As per Esther's request, the bodies of the sons of Haman were hanged on the gallows for all to see. In addition, the Jews defended themselves against their enemies and killed 75,000 enemies of Mordecai and his people.

These numbers are staggering. Over 75,000 enemies were killed.

Now, remember the instructions of Mordecai's decree. The Jews were supposed to defend themselves against anyone who would attack them according to Haman's decree. They were not to go out looking for trouble, but if trouble came, they were commanded to finish the job.

Remember how you felt when studying the chapter that told of Haman's death? Do you recall the feeling of victory, quickly followed by the sensation that there was more? The more was somewhat satisfied by the next story of victory—the story of Haman's ten sons being killed along with many hundreds of others who had risen up against the people of Mordecai. Such triumph! Such victory!

And yet, still the feeling of needing more remained—there was more to be done. I am aware that we live this story from a distance, through the pages, but we still feel it as we read it. Because God is illuminating it for our time, our spirits respond as if we were there. We are called to be Esther in our day. With that in mind, the further actions of Esther become vital instructions for us in our own Jesus revolution.

Esther would not quit; she could not—she was compelled to finish. She continued after many would have said the battle was over, that the enemy was routed. She just knew there was more. I believe the Spirit of God compelled her to press further.

As she did, the truth was revealed: the enemy was not gone. They had not been destroyed—they were simply hiding, perhaps waiting for a more advantageous time to make their move.

When Esther made her request, and the king followed by issuing the command to go again, the battle erupted once more. The hanging of the bodies of Haman's ten sons was a public display that flushed out the enemy. They were the bait, and 75,000 enemies appeared to take it. Can you imagine? Through the cipher of the code we understand that this was a demonic horde 75,000 strong.

What would have happened if Esther had quit early? What if she had not persisted? What would have become of the people of Mordecai if the enemy had been left alive? Remember, Esther was dealing with more than one man and his family. The battle of Haman and Mordecai is an ageless one. Esther had been confronted and challenged by the supernatural kingdom of darkness.

As long as there is even a sliver of a chance, the enemy of the ages keeps fighting. He is forever seeking a comeback.

It reminds me of those old cowboy movies. You know the ones I mean, where the good guy wears the white hat, the bad guy wears the black hat, and you just know the white hat will win in the end. But do you recall how often the bad guy had to be taken down before he would finally die? It seemed like he had a hundred lives. It wasn't until the man in the white hat went over and checked to make sure he was in fact dead that the audience could relax a little bit.

The enemy of our soul works in much the same way. He can seem to come back and come back and come back. While it may be that there is some new access window he has found, it is far more likely that we didn't finish the job in the first place. In truth, Esther was just finishing something that had been started centuries before she had even been born.

History Repeats Itself

Now this next truth is truly a revolutionary principle. It is a detail that suddenly makes phases one through ten come into focus. Remember, the phases are not about simple opportunity or human desires and wishes; they are strategies from the heart of God. God is timeless. He is the beginning and the end. He has always been and He will always be. Because He is eternal and because this revolution is His strategy, it should not surprise us that it transcends time. It should not be hard for us to accept that our phase one may have been activated as a response to someone else's failed phase ten.

Are you still with me? The promises of God throughout history have always endured the passing of time and generational transfer. Consider the promise God gave to Abraham, that he would be the father of a great nation. Abraham did not see it in his lifetime, but he sees it now. How about the promise of a Messiah that was delivered through the prophet Isaiah? He never saw Jesus in his lifetime here on the earth, but he sees Him now. Let me explain. We are spiritual beings and our life on this earth is just a small moment of the timeless, eternal journey. We are part of a far greater picture. Not only is God going to live forever, but we will as well. We must use our understanding of the eternal picture to discern that our destiny and calling may also be part of a bigger picture, a multi-generational picture and an historical placement.

Let's break down this historical placement in the life of Esther. What bigger picture was she born into? Follow me for a moment down a little bit of a genealogy trail. It is amazing to see in print the reality of a timeless God and His ongoing battle with the prince of darkness.

According to Esther 2:5-6, Esther and Mordecai were descendants of a man named Kish, who was from the tribe of Benjamin. Now the Kish mentioned here appears to have been a more recent descendant of Esther, falling into the timeline of the exile. But historians also believe that the genealogical line of Kish tracks back to a far earlier descendant of the same name and lineage. The genealogy of Kish leads us to his son, King Saul, the first king of Israel:

> There was a man of Benjamin whose name was Kish the son of Abiel, the son of Zeror, the son of Bechorath, the son of Aphiah, a Benjamite, a mighty man of power. And he had a choice and handsome son whose name was Saul. There was not a more handsome person than he among the children of Israel. From his shoulders upward he was taller than any of the people.
>
> —1 Samuel 9:1-2

Secondly, let us identify the lineage of Haman. According to Esther 3:1, Haman is the son of a man named Hammedatha who was an Agagite, a descendent of Agag. Agag was the king of the Amalekites, a fierce enemy of Israel in the days of King Saul.

Going back about six centuries, we are easily able to find the correlation between an ancient battle and the story of Esther that we've been studying. Suddenly, the fierce revulsion of Haman toward Mordecai makes a lot more sense:

> Samuel also said to Saul, "The Lord sent me to anoint you king over His people, over Israel. Now therefore, heed the voice of the words of the Lord. Thus says the Lord of hosts: 'I will punish Amalek for what he did to Israel, how he ambushed him on the way when he came up from Egypt. Now go and attack Amalek, and utterly destroy all that they have, and do not spare them. But kill both man and woman, infant and nursing child, ox and sheep, camel and donkey."
>
> —1 Samuel 15:1-3

What we see in the trail of history is that Esther was a descendant of Saul, the first king of Israel. Saul was a man of the people's choosing whom God allowed to be anointed over the kingdom. From the very beginning of Saul's reign he was mandated with a revolutionary mission: he was sent to deal with the descendants of Amalek who had been tormentors of Israel for many generations. Saul was asked complete phase ten for a previous generation.

Notice the similarity between the decree Mordecai drafted for the Jews in Esther 3, and the command of the Lord given to Saul in 1 Samuel 15:

> *By these letters the king permitted the Jews who were in every city to gather together and protect their lives--to destroy, kill, and annihilate all the forces of any people or province that would assault them, both the little children, and women, and to plunder their possessions.*
>
> —Esther 8:11

The decree of Mordecai was issued to the descendants of Saul. This was a repeat command, first issued to Saul six hundred years earlier. So why did it have to come again? Because Saul did not complete his mission.

King Saul failed as a ruler. It wasn't that Saul wasn't able to rule; the problem was that he ignored the command of the Lord and allowed pride to rule his heart. He didn't appreciate the value of the anointing, and he thought his own methods and standards were more important than God's:

> *And Saul attacked the Amalekites, from Havilah all the way to Shur, which is east of Egypt. He also took Agag king of the Amalekites alive, and utterly destroyed all the people with the edge of the sword. But Saul and the people spared Agag and the best of the sheep, the oxen, the fatlings, the lambs, and all that was good, and were unwilling to utterly*

destroy them. But everything despised and worthless, that
they utterly destroyed.

—1 Samuel 15:7-9

As we read the command of the Lord to King Saul, we see
that he is commanded to do one thing and one thing only: utterly destroy the Amalekites. They had already been adversaries
against God's people for many generations. In the days of Saul,
God was prepared to help Israel wipe them out completely.
All they needed to do was follow His command, but King Saul
didn't. He was unwilling to obey.

Saul's disobedience was no small thing in God's eyes:

Now the word of the Lord came to Samuel, saying, "I great-
ly regret that I have set up Saul as king, for he has turned
his back from following Me, and has not performed My
commandments." And it grieved Samuel, and he cried out
to the Lord all night.

—1 Samuel 15:10-11

Further on in the account (1 Samuel 15:12-21), we read
that not only did Saul spare King Agag— and evidently the royal
family—but he also kept the best of the plunder. He destroyed
the things that didn't appeal to him and kept the good stuff.
He chose to compromise on the command of God. The most
bizarre part of the account is that it appears that Saul actually
deceived himself into thinking that he had done the right thing.
His conscience was seared, and his own pride had convinced
him that compromising the command of the Lord was okay.

At the end of this story, the prophet Samuel killed Agag
himself. In fact, the Bible says he *"hacked Agag in pieces before*
the Lord" (1 Samuel 15:33). This is not the action of a savage
warrior but the action of a peacemaker. The prophet knew that
God was very serious about this, and he did his best to honour
God's command. But the damage had been done. A spirit of

rebellion and compromise had entered Israel, and history shows that a remnant of the house of Agag survived. Six centuries later, this same kingdom gave birth to Haman, a man who was born into a generational legacy of hatred toward God's people. He became host to a territorial spirit that was passed through his generational line.

As Esther and Mordecai came on the scene, they stepped into an old war. The decree to slaughter the Jews was far older than either of them. It was a decree that had been formed and declared hundreds of years before. Esther was dealing with demons that had been allowed access through a spirit of compromise.

I'm sure your heart aches, as mine does, at the reading of these words. The spirit of wisdom and revelation is illuminating the age-old mystery to our hearts. Through this revelation, we see and understand the necessity of this truth in our own day. The temptation of the lie of the enemy is laid out before us. It comes wrapped in a package, a buzz-word that is known to all in our time. The word we know and can easily recognize as a ploy of the enemy is "tolerance." Tolerance is just another name for compromise.

Tolerance is just another name for compromise.

Suddenly the request of the queen does not seem so bloodthirsty, does it? Her demand of a public display of the dead bodies of Haman's sons seems reasonable. Now, her desire to have a follow-up day of war to clean the slate makes sense.

It is interesting to note that in three separate places in Esther 9, it says, *"but they did not lay hand on the plunder"* (Esther 9: 10, 15, 16). Praise God! The people of Mordecai thoroughly and completely destroyed the enemy that had risen up against them and they did not take any of the plunder. They did not want anything the enemy might have to offer.

198 • Canada's Jesus Revolution

Esther did what her ancestor, King Saul, had not been willing to do. She finished the mission. She did not take compassion on the enemy. She did not allow them the opportunity of coming back. Also, she refused all of the enemy's goods—she refused to compromise.

The Final Piece

Earlier we looked at the promise of national intervention given to King Solomon. Let's look at it once again to pull out one final piece:

> *If My people who are called by My name will humble themselves, and pray and seek My face, and turn from their wicked ways, then I will hear from heaven, and I will forgive their sin and heal their land.*
> —2 Chronicles 7:14

What is the one piece we have overlooked until now? What part is yet required? We've talked about the calling, the humbling, the praying and the seeking—we must also address the wicked ways.

Many times we look to our nation and judge the sin and the sinners around us. We see the atrocities, the murders, the abortions, the deceptions and the abuses. It has been so easy to say that God can't move because there is sin in the land. But we must look carefully at where the promise is directed. It is a promise given to the people of God. The intervention of heaven isn't dependent on the lost turning from their wicked ways—it is dependent on the Church. We are called to be set apart as holy unto the Lord—we are called to operate in righteousness. A national call to holiness is preceded by a call to holiness within the Church.

> ## The intervention of heaven isn't dependent on the lost turning from their wicked ways—it's dependent on the Church.

Saul did almost all of what God had commanded him. He went to war. He defeated almost all of the enemy forces, but he saved the king. He destroyed most of the plunder, but he saved the stuff that appealed to him. He gave in to compromise.

Six hundred years later, Esther and her people faced the same command. But this time things turned out differently. Esther refused to compromise. She refused to let any of the enemy survive, and she and her people refused to take any of the plunder. They refused the delicacies of the enemy camp. They refused compromise. What was the result? True peace:

> *For Mordecai the Jew was second to King Ahasuerus, and was great among the Jews and well received by the multitude of his brethren, seeking the good of his people and speaking peace to all his countrymen.*
>
> —Esther 10:3

My fellow revolutionaries, we must know that if we begin this battle, we must also finish it! We must be committed to stay the course until it is done. Completely done. There is no room for compromise, no room for greed and no room for pride. We have been given a mission by our Commander-in-Chief, a mission that is for our good and for the good of our children and our children's children.

Esther completed her calling and saw her people set free from a demonic presence that had tormented them for hundreds of years. She closed a door that had been opened by compromise. She experienced the delight of victory, and saw the children of her generation free to live in peace and walk in the blessing of the Lord.

You and I have been called for such a time as this. We have been called to be a catalyst for change. We have been called to lay our lives on the line. We have been called to make a way for the King! We have been called to be revolutionaries!

Prayer

God, I am in awe of Your goodness, Your kindness, Your compassion, and Your great love for Your people. You are ageless and You truly do know the end from the beginning. I am reminded today that Your ways are perfect, and that Your commands are for my good. You desire to see Your people free. You desire to hear our invitation to reign in us and among us. Lord today, as much as it is my part to do, I invite You. I ask for Your rulership, Your guidance, and Your direction. Lord, I choose to believe what You say and I commit to do as You request. Your ways are higher than mine. So too, Your thoughts are higher than mine. I will listen. I will obey. I will not quit!

Lord, I am Yours!

CONCLUSION
CALL TO ACTION

As the story of Esther draws to a close, the story of the Bride of Christ in Canada begins. We too face insurmountable obstacles. We too live in a nation that has been infiltrated by the deception of the evil one. We too serve a God with a revolutionary strategy.

Perhaps you've been reading this book and you have been a bit overwhelmed by the call. Maybe you have felt honoured to be chosen or perhaps you have just felt afraid. Whatever state you find yourself in, the important thing to remember is that God simply desires a sincere, humble and obedient response: "Yes, Lord."

The call of a revolutionary is not easy, it is not comfortable, and it is not for the glory of self. If we have done the work of a revolutionary well, then what people will see and what they will hear is the name of Jesus. Jesus will awaken their hearts. He will give them hope. He will heal our land. My fellow revolutionaries, if we have done this correctly then the transformation will not be known as an Esther revolution, but always and only a Jesus revolution!

Esther does not represent any one of us; she represents all of us. She represents the Bride of Christ. Her great revolutionary mission was not about being made queen and becoming influential and famous. Esther's mission was to introduce Mordecai to a nation that desperately needed him. It is interesting to note that while the story starts with the entrance of a young queen, it ends with the name and fame of Mordecai. In truth, the story is really about him.

As we rise up to take our place in the revolutionary call of Canada, we must remember that our calling is from a higher realm. We did not choose Him but He chose us. It is His doing. The history of our lives should always openly be read as His-story.

We don't fight for our nation because she needs it. We don't stand against injustice because it bothers us. We don't pursue change because we are frustrated with what is presently happening around us. The true call of a revolutionary is about seeing God's will done, and His desire released in our nation. It is about pursuing the heart of our King. He loves Canada. He has a plan for her, and He is inviting us to partner with Him in calling her to transformation, calling her to walk out her prophetic destiny.

God is calling *you* to action, for this hour, for Canada. Heed the inner stirring. Listen for God's commands. Obey the Commander-in-Chief's instructions, regardless of personal cost.

What would have happened if Esther had not heard from God? What if she hadn't obeyed? What if she had followed the example of Saul so many years before and succumbed to compromise? What if she had decided the cost was too great?

Every act of obedience from every revolutionary is vital to Canada's transformation: praying and interceding; sharing the Good News with family, friends, coworkers and neighbours; being elected to governmental positions; writing emails, letters, books, or songs—whatever God puts in *your* heart to do.

Don't hold back. Do not be deceived by the enemy. Do not try to understand your orders, or try to figure them all out—just obey!

I stand with you today as a passionately committed part of Canada's Jesus revolution—for such a time as this! Please join me in declaring once again: **God, I am Yours!**

O Canada
Public Domain

Verse 1

O Canada! Our home and native land!
True patriot love in all thy sons command.
With glowing hearts we see thee rise, The True North strong and free.
From far and wide, O Canada, We stand on guard for thee.
God keep our land glorious and free!
O Canada, we stand on guard for thee,
O Canada, we stand on guard for thee.

Verse 4

Ruler supreme, Who hearest humble prayer, Hold our dominion, in Thy loving care.
Help us to find, O God, in Thee, A lasting rich reward.
As waiting for the better day, We ever stand on guard.
God keep our land, glorious and free.
O Canada, we stand on guard for thee,
O Canada, we stand on guard for thee!

ABOUT THE AUTHOR

Having come to the knowledge of Christ at a young age, Charlotte Quist has dedicated her life to discovering the Creator and mining the truths hidden in His Word. She has faithfully served the Body of Christ alongside Wayne, her high-school sweetheart and husband of over twenty years, who operates his own successful sound production company. Together they have raised two beautiful daughters and recently had the joy of welcoming two sons-in-law into the family.

Many years of lay ministry eventually led Charlotte toward ordination and a position as Worship Pastor/Women's Ministry Director for over twelve years. What began as a calling to worship ministry as a teenager developed into a lifelong mission that branched out to include international teaching, preaching, team development and spearheading interdenominational workshops and conferences.

Her love of the truth has lead her from being a student to becoming a sought-out conference speaker, radio preacher and Bible College teacher throughout Canada, Thailand, Haiti and the Philippines. She has developed and written college-level courses on a variety of topics, including spiritual warfare, discovering your destiny, and praise and worship. She has also written numerous Bible studies including *Enter His Gates – A guide to the temple*, *Proverbs 31 – A Woman that Wins*, and a woman's devotional titled *In Her Shoes*. *Canada's Jesus Revolution* is her first published work.

There is no room for grey in Charlotte's black-and-white, prophetically accurate messages. Her passion for God's truth is easily heard in her words, while her humourous, straight-shooting delivery provides easy-to-understand and relevant revelations of the Word. Her heart burns to see the Church of Canada raise up to take her place among the nations. Empowered by Holy Spirit, Charlotte practises what she preaches, daily laying down her life saying, "God, I am yours!"

For more information or booking inquiries please go to:
www.charlottequist.ca